Aggressive Behavior
and the Rosenzweig
Picture–Frustration Study

AGGRESSIVE BEHAVIOR AND THE ROSENZWEIG PICTURE-FRUSTRATION STUDY

Saul Rosenzweig
Washington University
St. Louis

PRAEGER PUBLISHERS
Praeger Special Studies

New York　•　London　•　Sydney　•　Toronto

Library of Congress Cataloging in Publication Data

Rosenzweig, Saul, 1907–
  Aggressive behavior and the Rosenzweig picture-
frustration study.

  Bibliography: p.
  1. Rosenzweig picture-frustration test.
2. Aggressiveness (Psychology)—Testing.   I. Title.
BF698.8.R6R67   155.2'84   78-18200
ISBN 0-03-045656-8

PRAEGER SPECIAL STUDIES
383 Madison Avenue, New York, N.Y., 10017,
U.S.A.
Published in the United States of America in 1978
by Praeger Publishers,
A Division of Holt, Rinehart and Winston, CBS Inc.
89 038 987654321
© 1978 by Saul Rosenzweig
Printed in the United States of America

CONTENTS

PREFACE

This volume is a comprehensive and critical report on the research which has been accomplished with the Rosenzweig Picture-Frustration (P-F) Study over a 40-year period. It includes some discussion of the work in experimental psychodynamics which underlies and led to the construction of the instrument. For the P-F originated as a means to further experimental investigation as well as for more immediate personnel or clinical application. Both these objectives are still relevant and are constantly in view in the chapters which follow.

The universality of frustration and the perennial interest in aggressive behavior give this volume its reason for existence. It is hoped that the investigations conducted with such a broad variety of subjects in widely dispersed cultures and countries will add something of significance to the understanding and solution of the complex problems inherent in personal and group conflict. Since the instrument has found worldwide acceptance and exists in parallel standardized forms in many nationalities, the opportunity exists for a broadening and intensification of the burgeoning research which it has already sparked on cross-cultural differences in aggressive reactions to frustration. The utility of the device with individuals is attested by its unabated persistence despite various assaults on other tests that appear as threats to privacy. The idiodynamic context in which the P-F is embedded renders it relatively immune in this regard.

Though the focus is on the P-F Study, it should be observed that many of the concepts and methods employed in the consideration of reliability, validity, and dynamics have a wider significance. For example, the problems of reliability and validity of projective and semiprojective methods are still in need of clarification, and it is hoped that the guidelines employed for the evaluation of the P-F will help toward solving the problems of cognate techniques. Even more important, perhaps, is the obvious usefulness of the technique not merely as an assessment device but as an exemplar of certain dynamic concepts which it helps to clarify and to promote.

In Part I the current status of the P-F Study is surveyed. The definition of aggression and a synoptic view of the P-F leads into a critical discussion of its reliability and validity. A survey of the various applications of the P-F (pragmatic validity) will also be found here. In

Part II a brief chronological history of the instrument and the research from which it originated are presented. Then follows a topical guide to P-F research with a citation index. This index is geared to the bibliographies in Part III where all the relevant literature by author and title is listed.

Saul Rosenzweig
St. Louis, Missouri

ACKNOWLEDGMENTS

The one to whom I am uniquely indebted in the publication of this work is my wife, Louise. With her the P-F idea was conceived, and this fruition of it is preeminently due to her constant collaboration.

Numerous others have contributed to the research on and with the P-F Study over the past 40 years. Of those who have made highly significant contributions in the writer's laboratories the following are gratefully singled out for mention: Stuart Adelman, who is first not only alphabetically but in the extent and the recency of his assistance; Robert B. Bell, Stephen H. Braun, Helen Jane Clarke, Edith E. Fleming, David J. Ludwig, Esther Lee Mirmow, and Seymour B. Sarason. All these assistants, and others not named here, appear as authors or coauthors in the bibliographies included in this volume.

In the research outside the United States, the following investigators have made important contributions, both in the adaptation and standardization of the instrument in their respective countries or cultures and in other substantive investigations: Pierre Pichot and Charles Kramer in France; Erna Duhm in Germany; Franco Ferracuti and Rodolfo Nencini in Italy; Ake Bjerstedt in Sweden; Udo Rauchfleisch in Switzerland; Nuria Cortada de Kohan in Argentina; Eva Nick in Brazil; Udai Pareek in India; and Katsuzo Hayashi and Tsuyoshi Ichitani in Japan.

Acknowledgment is due the many individuals in schools at every level, in clinics and hospitals, courts and prisons, business and industry, who contributed subjects or themselves served as subjects for the work in progress. For unstinting and devoted secretarial assistance I am grateful to Lorraine M. Constantine.

The following journals have given permission for the adaptation or reproduction of previously published material: *Aggressive Behavior, Journal of Clinical Psychology,* and *Journal of Personality Assessment.* I want, in particular, to note the kindness of Dr. and Mrs. Walter G. Klopfer, who edit the last-named periodical.

To my friend Kenneth L. Nabors, Chief Reference Librarian of the Washington University Olin Library, I am grateful for his expert and generous help.

Part One

Current Status of the Picture-Frustration Study

1 Overview: Aggressive Behavior and Its Assessment

AGGRESSION DEFINED

Discussion of aggression by psychologists in recent times has been marked by two fallacies. One of these equates aggression with hostility or destructiveness. This view ignores a broader conception that essentially agrees with common sense and conceives of aggression as assertive action. There is a problem to be solved, and in attempting to cope with it the individual asserts himself either constructively or destructively: constructively, if the solution is achieved without harm to other individuals or their property; destructively, if the solution entails such harm. While it is true that at times the achievement of a constructive solution can appear to a competitor as destructive of his interests, the behavior itself is not essentially affected by this interpretation. In any event, there are, on the one hand, clear-enough instances of assertive action that are constructive without any intended threat to others and, on the other hand, instances in which coping deliberately involves such damage to other persons or property. The ambiguous intermediate case should not obscure this patent distinction that justifies a broad conception of aggression in which it is no longer equated with hostility or destructiveness alone. It is this broad conception which is adopted here.

The other fallacy concerns the role of antecedent frustration in eliciting aggression. Here one is concerned again with a broadening of the base, this time with respect to aggression which is destructive. While it is true that frustration may instigate hostility or destructive aggression, it is not justifiable by present knowledge to limit the origin of hostile aggression to such antecedents. There is at least some evidence to suggest that hostility may arise sui generis. While this view is not universally endorsed by students of behavior, there is sufficient difference of opinion to warrant caution in defining the role of frustration in eliciting aggression. And since frustration can be conceived as either primary (in the mere fact that a need exists) or secondary (when an obstacle is interposed in the process of proceeding to the final stage of goal-directed behavior), frustration itself can be regarded as defining a problem situation.

The end result would be that aggression conceived as initiated by a problem is generically some form of assertive or coping behavior, which may then be either constructive or destructive in effect. Aggression can then no longer be limited to something negative or hostile nor can hostility itself invariably require an antecedent state of frustration.

With this orientation a general definition of aggression may now be offered.* It is proposed that, from a multilevel approach to behavior, aggression be conceptualized to include: (1) generic assertiveness in apposite life situations; (2) neural mechanisms that subserve such behaviors; (3) physiological conditions that mediate or promote these behaviors. Number Three is usefully studied by observing the effects of chemical preparation (drugs). Number Two may be investigated by brain stimulation and ablation. But Number One, concerned with overt behavior as observed, is fundamental to all phases of aggression. It is this broadest parameter which will be highlighted in the present discussion.

To explain *assertiveness* as the generic meaning of aggression, it should first be noted that "aggression" has come to have a negative connotation in many technical discussions though it still retains a broader meaning in everyday use. Since there are terms like "hostility" and "violence" to describe the particulars of negative aggression, there appears to be good reason to retain the broader potential that aggressive behavior can involve. It is hence maintained that assertiveness be regarded as the essential component of aggression. In keeping with its etymology, aggression would generically mean stepping or moving forward to achieve goals and overcome obstacles. Originating in asser-

---

*The rest of this section was initially prepared as a contribution to the Workshop on the Definition of Aggression, First Congress of the International Society for Research on Aggression, Toronto, Canada, August 18, 1974. (See Rosenzweig 1977a.) The present version is the same in substance but revised in its details.

tiveness, aggression is thus defined as potentially including constructive action as regards the goal to be achieved; the means employed in such action remains by definition neutral. The means may then be further described as either *constructive*, when there is no entailed damage or injury to other individuals or objects, or *destructive*, i.e., to the extent that other individuals or objects are injured or destroyed by the behavior. This distinction between constructive and destructive aggression will be maintained hereafter.

It is obvious that, at this stage of knowledge, a consensual definition of aggression is needed to facilitate communication among investigators and to reduce confusion in research activities. Moreover, at this time the definition should be denotative; it should concentrate on those recognized forms of behavior that are defined by the life situations in which they occur. This approach is avowedly phenotypic. It assumes that at a riper stage of knowledge a more genotypic definition will be possible.

The following further definition proceeds by classification. The classification does not attempt strictly to define stimuli. Settings, as they are here designated, appear to be sufficiently precise and, at any rate, are as much as can be reasonably offered according to present knowledge. In the last analysis it will probably turn out that, whether regarded as stimuli or as settings, the instigating triggers of aggression in any given instance will reflect the unique (idiodynamic) demands of the subject at the moment.

The life situations in which aggression has been described in the scientific literature include the following (see Figure 1):

1. *Privation,* which embraces (a) the frustration of vital needs and (b) that produced by inner (endopsychic) conflicts. In the former, some interference with the need for security from pain or injury, for air, food, water, sexual expression, parental response, etc., is involved. In the latter, frustration is induced by conflict between two incompatible needs; e.g., the need for sexual response and the need for security or inviolacy (freedom from pain, shame, guilt). The justification for characterizing such conflict as "privation" is found in the fact that the individual in such a condition is deprived of the "peace of mind"—the relatively tensionless state—that was present before the conflict or would exist without it. It should be incidentally observed that this kind of conflict is not to be confused with the type of social conflict considered in the next subdivision.

2. *Conflict* (social), which embraces competition between rivals for specific food supplies, for living space, etc., at a given time. While the

FIGURE 1

PHENOTYPIC SETTINGS OF AGGRESSION

PRIVATION	CONFLICT (SOCIAL)	VICTIMIZATION
FRUSTRATION OF VITAL NEEDS	SITUATION-SPECIFIC COMPETITION	PREDATOR – PREY RELATIONS
FRUSTRATION BY INNER (ENDOPSYCHIC) CONFLICT	INTRAGROUP RIVALRY FOR DOMINANCE	VANDALISM PER SE
REACTION: NEED-PERSISTIVE/ ETHO-DEFENSIVE	RESOLUTION: CONSTRUCTIVE/ DESTRUCTIVE	PROVENANCE: DERIVATIVE / INTRINSIC ?

same ultimate dissatisfactions may be present here as in division 1, the difference lies in the presence of an external competitor for the means to satisfaction. Related to such situation-specific competition is the state of affairs created by claims to abiding (relatively permanent) positions of dominance within the group (dominance hierarchies, family organization).

Reactions to privation (frustration) may be viewed as *need-persistive* or *etho-defensive,* just as conflict resolution may be viewed as *constructive* or *destructive.* All these behaviors are, of course, forms of aggression. In previous writing, the distinction between constructive and destructive aggression has been delineated as need-persistence (in which the striving initiated by a need persists toward the goal despite an intervening obstacle) and ego-defense (in which the behavior induced by a frustrating obstacle becomes hostile). Such hostility can be turned outward, against the external world (other persons or objects), to be designated as "extrapunitive"; turned inward, against the self, termed "intropunitive"; or turned off in a conciliatory fashion, called "impunitive". But in the present framework the designation *ego-defense* is replaced by *etho-defense* because the intent is to describe defenses of the total organization of behavior in the manner that ethology studies it. Thus renamed, this hostile type of aggression can be extended to the behavior of lower animals, where the concept of ego or self is not clearly appropriate. In essence, however, the distinction between need-persistence and etho-defense still points to the difference between a constructive solution to frustration or conflict and a destructive or hostile one.

It should, however, be observed that need-persistence, though constructive in its initial impetus, can become destructive in situations where the needs of others represent the obstacle. In other words, need-persistence in the face of a contravalent need-persistence constitutes conflict, with all the attendant possibilities of hostility and destructiveness. It is, in fact, just this type of phenotypic situation which tends to confound the distinction between constructive and destructive aggression. What from the standpoint of person number 1 may appear (subjectively) to be constructive need-persistence may, from the standpoint of number 2, intent upon the satisfaction of his needs, appear to be incorrigible, if not hostile, contrariness.

As regards conflict (social), destructive resolution treats the situation as an adversary contest—a fight between opponents one of whom must destroy, injure, or demean the other. In constructive resolution the situation is treated as a shared problem which can be solved with mutual benefits—benefits that exploit the advantages of cooperating diversity. Such constructive resolution is found in many animal species where hierarchies of dominance are established to facilitate social organization and which, in turn, favor group survival by reducing intragroup tension and augmenting cooperation in day-to-day living. Much of the ritualistic dominance behavior in such groups illustrates the manner in which constructive conflict resolution reduces injury to group members and increases the efficiency of group functioning.

(3) *Victimization* includes two types of situation. In the first, one organism is the prey; i.e., the victim, of another, the predator. In the wild, predator-prey relationships are motivated by survival—by natural conditions in which certain organisms can survive only by destroying and devouring others. In these circumstances, the aggression involved merges into privation since it is motivated by the frustration of survival needs. There is a second subdivision of victimization where the survival aspect is not so clear. Here the victim is an object of sheer destructiveness, and aggression then appears to be equivalent to vandalism. Such vandalism may merge into or out of predator-prey relationships; it may, in fact, derive from them in ways not presently understood; i.e., by phylogenetic or ontogenetic short-circuiting. But some theorists would take exception to any such attempted derivation and would insist upon observed vandalism as existing per se on some intrinsic, innate basis.

The P-F Study as an Assessment Tool

With the total scope of aggression now in view, the more limited range of the Rosenzweig Picture-Frustration (P-F) Study may be defined. As will presently appear, the P-F Study concentrates upon the first two classes of phenotypic settings presented in Figure 1: privation and conflict. Moreover, it explores the modes of personal reaction to these situations by verbal means—verbal stimuli eliciting verbal responses. Obviously, the technique is thus limited in its assessment potential, and the extent of this limitation is one of the problems of reliability and validity that the investigator faces. But it should be noted at the outset that, though the title of the instrument focuses on frustration, the assumption is not made that frustration is invariably an antecedent of aggression or that aggression necessarily implies some prior condition of frustration.

The writer's earliest formulations of the frustration problem (Rosenzweig, 1934b, 1938b) preceded the well-known monograph on frustration and aggression by the Yale group (*Dollard, Doob, Miller,*

Mowrer, and *Sears, 1939).** Moreover, it differed from the Yale formulation in some crucial respects. For one thing, it included nonhostile impunitiveness as a possible alternative to outwardly and inwardly directed hostility; the Yale view conceived the aggressive consequences of frustration as exclusively hostile. Again, it defined aggression broadly to embrace both constructive (need-persistive) and destructive (ego-defensive) consequences of frustration. It should, however, be noted that this latter distinction was not explicitly delineated until somewhat later (Rosenzweig, 1941).

The P-F Study resulted from experimental research originally intended to refine certain of the clinically derived concepts of psychoanalysis, for example, repression (compare Rosenzweig, 1937a, 1960). From this research there emerged a dynamic formulation in which frustration served as the nexus. In contradistinction to many psychoanalytic concepts, frustration can be defined operationally without losing clinical relevance or, more generally, relevance to everyday behavior.

The P-F Study is a semiprojective technique which combines features of the word-association method of *Galton (1879–1880)* and *Jung (1918 [1906])* with the Thematic Apperception Test (TAT) of *Morgan* and *Murray (1935).* More intrinsically it represents a convergence of the three fundamental approaches to the psychodynamics of human behavior: systematic research, psychometric method, and clinical insight. For the P-F, systematic research means experimental psychodynamics that focuses on universal or nomothetic norms, for example, the principles of Types and Directions of Aggression. Psychometric method means statistical analysis that yields group or demographic norms, for example, the Group Conformity Rating (GCR) and the percentile norms for the P-F aggression categories. Clinical insights derive from idiodynamic analysis, for example, Trends extracted from scrutiny of the record of the individual subject. The P-F combines these three kinds of norms operationally, but in such fashion that the idiodynamics of the examinee can be expressed by him and can be read out of the protocol by the experienced examiner [Rosenzweig, 1951a, 1958].†

---

*All references cited in italics, as in this case, will be found in the Supplementary References list rather than in P-F References by Author.

†In this context it should be made clear that *idiodynamic* is not to be confused with *idiographic. Idiographic* is customarily contrasted with *nomothetic* in approaches to the psychology of the individual and his *traits,* with the emphasis upon the size of the *N* in the universe or population under consideration. *Idiodynamic* refers to the idioverse, that is, the given individual's world of *events,* which generates its own norms. Hence, norms, not traits, become paramount, and to idiodynamic norms are added the norms of the group (demographic) and those of the total possible universe of concerned individuals (nomothetic).

DESCRIPTION OF THE INSTRUMENT

The Rosenzweig Picture-Frustration (P-F) Study or, by its full name—The Picture-Association Method for Assessing Reactions to Frustration—represents a limited projective procedure for disclosing certain patterns of response to everyday stress that are broadly applicable in both normal and abnormal adjustment (Rosenzweig, 1945). There are three Forms: for Children, ages 4–13; for Adolescents, ages 12–18; and for Adults, ages 18 and over. The material of the technique is a series of 24 cartoonlike pictures, each depicting an everyday, interpersonal frustrating situation, presented to the subject in a self-administering leaflet (the examination blank). The figure at the left of each item is shown saying certain words which either help to describe the frustration of the other individual involved or which of themselves actually frustrate him. The person on the right is always shown with a blank caption box (balloon) above his head. Facial features and other expressions of personality have been deliberately omitted to facilitate projective structuring. The subject is instructed to examine the situations one at a time and to write in the balloon the first reply of the anonymous person on the right that occurs to him. In some cases the situation is ego-blocking; some obstruction, personal or impersonal, impedes, disappoints, deprives, or otherwise directly thwarts the pictured person. In the other cases, super-ego-blocking is portrayed: the individual is accused, insulted, or otherwise incriminated by another person.

Competent use of the P-F requires familiarity with the *Basic Manual* (Rosenzweig, 1978a) which pertains in common to all three Forms. In addition to this digest of information as to rationale, reliability and validity, a manual *Supplement* for each level provides particulars on standardization, scoring samples, and norms, with illustrative protocols to guide interpretation.

RATIONALE: BASIC P-F SCORING CONSTRUCTS

The P-F Study is derived conceptually from the principles of frustration theory; on the technical side it follows, in part, the projective methodology. Formally it is less free than projective methods such as the Thematic Apperception Test because its stimulus situations are deliberately more structured. The responses elicited are both narrower in range and briefer in content. The P-F has therefore sometimes been called a limited, semiprojective technique. One favorable implication of its circumscribed character is the advantage offered of handling its results on an objective, statistical basis. To the student of personality it has therefore appealed as a means for investigating both frustration theory and the conceptual basis of the projective techniques.

Frustration Theory

As a stimulus to growth, frustration is an ingredient of all behavior. In abnormal conditions the importance of stress to the origin and nature of illness would be difficult to overestimate. In specialized forms frustration enters into most, if not all, creative activity. Any instrument that contributes to an appraisal of the effects of frustration in the individual is therefore naturally of very broad interest.

Frustration theory assumes the unity of the organism. It implements this point of view by adopting frustration as a centrally orienting concept and by ordering to it, in operational and experimental terms, many of the insights derived from psychodynamics (Rosenzweig, 1944). The theory includes three levels of psychobiological defense: the cellular or immunological, the autonomic or emergency, and the cortical or ego-defensive. The interrelationships of these levels in the unified functioning of the organism provide the key to both normal and maladjusted behavior. A general approach to normal, abnormal, and supernormal behavior is implicit in the previously indicated continuum: frustration-growth-creativity.

Frustration is defined as occurring whenever the organism encounters an obstacle or obstruction en route to the satisfaction of a need. But this definition implies a prior recognition that all behavioral response is response to minimal irritation (primary frustration) which is accompanied by tension. Tension is inherent in the very process of life behavior. When (as noted) an obstacle explicit enough to require special effort breaches the horizon, an adventitious increase of tension occurs. Frustration, as invoked in the description of behavior, is usually of this secondary or adventitious order. In frustration theory it is hypothesized that when such adventitious stress occurs aggression in some form is entailed.

Aggression Constructs

To define the reactions of the subject in the frustrating situations represented in the P-F, scores are assigned to each response under two

TABLE 1: Constructs of Reaction to Frustration

DIRECTION OF AGGRESSION ↓	TYPE OF AGGRESSION		
	Obstacle-Dominance (O-D)	Ego-Defense (E-D) (Etho-Defense)	Need-Persistence (N-P)
Extraggression (E-A)	E' (Extrapeditive): The presence of the frustrating obstacle is insistently pointed out.	E (Extrapunitive): Blame, hostility, etc., are turned against some person or thing in the environment. <u>E</u>: In this variant of E, the subject aggressively denies that he is responsible for some offense with which he is charged.	e (Extrapersistive): A solution for the frustrating situation is emphatically expected of someone else.
Intraggression (I-A)	I' (Intropeditive): The frustrating obstacle is construed as not being frustrating or even as in some way beneficial; or, in some instances, the subject emphasizes the extent of his embarrassment at being involved in instigating another's frustration.	I (Intropunitive): Blame, censure, etc., are directed by the subject upon himself. <u>I</u>: A variant of I in which the subject admits his guilt but denies any essential fault by referring to unavoidable circumstances.	i (Intropersistive): Amends are offered by the subject, usually from a sense of guilt, to solve the problem.
Imaggression (M-A)	M' (Impeditive): The obstacle in the frustrating situation is minimized almost to the point of denying its existence.	M (Impunitive): Blame for the frustration is evaded altogether, the situation being regarded as unavoidable; in particular, the "frustrating" individual is absolved.	m (Impersistive): Expression is given to the hope that time or normally expected circumstances will bring about a solution of the problem; patience and conformity are characteristic.

main headings: Direction of Agression and Type of Aggression (see Table 1). Included under Direction of Aggression are extraggression (E-A), in which aggression is turned onto the environment; intraggression (I-A), in which it is turned by the subject upon himself; and imaggression (M-A), in which aggression is evaded in an attempt to gloss over the frustration. It is as though, to use a paraphrase, extraggression turns aggression out, intraggression turns it in, and imaggression turns it off. Included under Type of Aggression are obstacle-dominance (O-D), in which the barrier that occasions the frustration stands out in the response; ego- or etho-defense (E-D), in which the organizing capacity of the subject predominates to defend its integrity; and need-persistence (N-P), in which the solution of the frustrating problem is emphasized by pursuing the goal despite the obstacle.

It is advisable, possibly preferable, to substitute "etho-defense" for "ego-defense" (used in earlier P-F writing), so that defense against the disruption of organized behavior in species other than man can be included under this rubric. It is, of course, obvious that not only etho-defense but obstacle-dominance and need-persistence (and probably the three directions of aggression) are applicable beyond homo sapiens.

From the combination of the six interrelated *categories* there result for each P-F item nine possible scoring *factors* (and two variants, E and I). These factors serve for the actual scores assigned. However, the categories are the basic constructs of the P-F Study and are regarded as more essential than the factors for psychological interpretation and for the assessment of reliability and validity. There are norms for both the categories and the factors.

It is crucial to note that the constructs of the P-F do not involve types (or traits) of personality. Instead, types of reaction or behavior, available to everyone, are posited. The sample of verbal responses elicited by the projective device attempts to assess the more characteristic (not necessarily permanent or universal) reaction types used by the subject.

It is important also to repeat that aggression in the P-F and in the constructs on which it is based is not necessarily negative in quality. Need-persistence represents a *constructive* (sometimes creative) form of aggression while ego (etho)-defense is frequently *destructive* (of others or of oneself) in import. This point is emphasized because in many theories of aggression this distinction is overlooked, and aggression is then practically synonymous with hostility or destructiveness.

Common parlance, when not influenced by psychoanalytic or other psychological conceptualization, is closer to the broader usage of the term *aggression* upon which the P-F Study depends.

It should, however, be noted that need-persistence is not an unmitigated good and is not in all circumstances constructive. While in its initiation such behavior may appear to the subject to be merely constructive, it can lead to conflict, with attendant destructiveness, in situations where the needs of others constitute the obstacle. When need-persistence confronts a contravalent need-persistence the distinction between constructive and destructive aggression becomes blurred; the behaviors involved may merge into hostility from the standpoint of one or both parties. In the interpretation of P-F results this possibility should be taken into account, particularly when the need-persistence score is markedly elevated.

Individual responses are scored by employing either one or two of the factors according to the phraseology of the response. Deep interpretations are avoided in the scoring because only a descriptive analysis is intended. Scoring samples are available in the P-F manuals to aid in the making of decisions. When the item scores have been obtained, the scoring blank is compiled. The item scores are tallied by component to obtain percentages of the six scoring categories which occur in the protocol of the subject. A Group Conformity Rating (GCR) for certain criterion items makes it possible to indicate in one gross figure the subject's tendency to agree in his responses with the modal responses of the normal population used for standardization purposes. Patterns that summarize the predominance of the scoring factors in the individual record are also derived. Finally, Trends are calculated to show whether the subject modifies his reactions to frustration as he proceeds from the first half to the second half of the Study. Here one is concerned with the individual's reactions to his own previous reactions, for example, guilt as manifested in increased intropunitiveness after earlier indulgence in extrapunitiveness. Illustrative protocols that demonstrate both the scoring of individual items and the compilation of the scoring blank are available in the manuals and in other sources (Rosenzweig, 1945, 1950g, 1960, 1977a, 1978b; Rosenzweig and Kogan, 1949).

Needless to state, accuracy in scoring is essential if the P-F Study is to be adequately employed. For most clinical purposes it suffices for the examiner to become familiar with the scoring rubrics (which must, of course, be effected through experience with the contents of actual protocols) and to supplement this skill by a conscientious use of the scoring samples available for every item in all three forms (or levels). By matching the actual given response against these standard samples the vast majority of responses can be accurately scored. The remainder will be evaluated in terms of the best understanding of the scoring constructs that the examiner can command. But for more serious research purposes this individual procedure needs to be modified to achieve the necessary scoring reliability. A simple and efficient method is as follows: two or more examiners, experienced in the use of the P-F, independently score each protocol on separate scoring blanks. Each examiner naturally uses the individual method described above. Next, the two sets of scores are compared. If the examiners are properly qualified and have been sufficiently conscientious, they will have achieved agreement in approximately 80 percent of their scores (Clarke, Rosenzweig, and Fleming, 1947) The remaining three to five items will then be segregated for scoring in consultation. In the end, by the use of this procedure, consensual scoring will be achieved, based upon the conferences which originally entered into the compilation of the standardized scoring samples as supplemented by the similar consultation of the two or more current investigators. In most of the recent research performed in our laboratories, this is the procedure which has been employed.

Interpretation

The interpretation of the P-F Study is patterned on the concepts of frustration theory (previously reviewed), as fortified by empirically obtained norms. It is important to recognize, as a general principle, that all the reactions to frustration anticipated in the P-F Study are intrinsically neither normal nor abnormal; that is, they are neutral. The appropriateness of the projective response could be determined only by knowing all the circumstances of an actual, corresponding situation. However, to determine the bias of the subject's stereotypes, as these are elicited projectively in circumstances in which he is free to respond without the restrictions of real conditions, one can employ group norms for comparison with the subject's scores. This social criterion of normality figures in the interpretive standards for the GCR and for the percentages of P-F categories and factors. Agreement with the standardization group is taken as one criterion of healthy adjustment.

It should, however, be further noted that the social criterion is not the only one involved in the P-F Study. The interpretation of the total protocol, in which the interrelationships of the various quantitative scores and the qualitative indications in the individual record are scrutinized, also involves an idiodynamic criterion of normality, that is, the particular economy of intraindividual organization. It is therefore understandable that the P-F is adapted less to categorizing individuals by psychiatric diagnosis than to providing an idiodynamic interpretation of the individual personality (Rosenzweig, 1951a).

In keeping with the cautions to be discussed under the section on administration, it is crucially important to consider, when one is making interpretations, the probable level of the subject's responses. Careful individual administration of the instrument is therefore necessary for optimal clinical application. Needless to say, the clinical experience of the examiner and his knowledge of personality and psychodynamics also set limits to the validity of the findings. When the P-F is included in a full psychodiagnostic battery, its interpretation is fortified by comparative analysis.

By and large, a representative P-F protocol may contribute knowledge of the subject's characteristic modes of response to frustration and the nature of his recourse to aggression. Deviations from the percentage norms for the various P-F categories aid in such interpretation. On a similar basis it is possible to infer the degree of the subject's healthy adjustment to his group from scrutiny of the GCR. However, the most telling interpretations are those which are derived from the interrelationships of the various scoring components, which, among other things, throw light upon the subject's frustration tolerance. The hypothetical criteria for this last kind of inference have been examined in the context of (therapeutic) behavior change (Rosenzweig, 1950a).

METHODS AND PROBLEMS
OF ADMINISTRATION

The P-F may be administered either to individuals or to groups but the former method is preferred since more careful administration, including the important Inquiry, is thus readily possible (Rosenzweig, 1960). The Study is printed in an eight-page examination blank, of which the first page is devoted to instructions; each of the next six shows four of the previously described situations. In the standard procedure the examiner hands the subject an examination blank and reads over the instructions with him. The leaflet is then opened, the first item is read aloud, and the subject asked, as a demonstration, what answer first comes to his mind. If the subject at this point inquires whether he should respond as he himself would do, the examiner replies, "not necessarily": the answer may or may not correspond to what the subject would actually say. The subject is then instructed again that he is supposed to write down the very first words which come to his mind as being said by the person in the picture. When the subject produces this answer, he is told to write it in the caption box. The demonstration is important in order to reinforce the instruction, particularly with regard to the subject's indicating the very first response that he thinks would be given by the anonymous figure on the right in each item. Subsequent to the administration, the subject is told to proceed with the rest of the items in order, silently, by himself. After all the balloons are filled in, the examination blank is picked up and the examiner records the total time spent by the subject in completing it.

As is implicit in the above, the written method of self-administration is to be followed wherever possible. If an oral method is necessary because the subject is an illiterate adult or a child who is not yet able to read and write, a separate examination blank should still be used with each subject. In this way one can best simulate the standardized procedure, which was deliberately designed to encourage projection and to avoid the censoring of responses in a face-to-face confrontation.* The standard procedure is usually possible with the majority of children eight years old or over. With younger children the examiner reads the instructions in the leaflet while the child looks on. The P-F is called a "game" to be played. The game is to write in the empty space the first answer you think the other person would give in each of the situations pictured. The first page is then turned and the examiner proceeds as indicated above. However, the examiner writes at the dictation of the child (or the illiterate adult) the answers given for each item. All answers are written in the examination blank as the subject looks on. But it should be emphasized that whenever possible the subject should read and write for himself since experimentation with matched groups has shown that oral administration is apt to increase censorship in the direction of polite or acceptable answers (Rosenzweig, 1951b). This possible effect of the oral administration is perhaps less pronounced at ages four to seven, and, in any event, the norms for these earlier ages were of necessity established by such administration.

It is assumed that the subject unconsciously or consciously identi-

---

*In the movie *A Clockwork Orange* (*Kubrick, 1972*, reel 15) a variant of the P-F Study is introduced to evaluate the effects of the aversive-conditioning therapy used with the hero. This application of the P-F, made without consulting the present writer, is misleading because it employs an oral administration by means of a slide projector. The author of the original version of the story (*Burgess, 1963*, pp. 180–181) did not make this mistake; his "doctor vecks" used a booklet.

fies himself with the frustrated person portrayed on the right in each pictured situation. However, the kind and extent of projective response elicited by the technique depend upon the subject's set—his self-instruction. To determine this self-instruction—and also to obtain cues for more adequate scoring of the necessarily brief responses—the examiner conducts an inquiry after the subject has filled in all the balloons. The subject is requested to read back what he has written or what has been written at his dictation, so that the examiner will be sure to understand, while the latter casually interrupts, with nonleading questions, to gain more information about brief or ambiguous responses which might present scoring difficulties. For example, tonal inflections are noted if these indicate sarcasm, petulance, humility, and so on, relevant in the scoring yet to be done.* At the very end an effort is made to determine at what level or levels the subject has identified himself with the anonymous frustrated figures in the pictured situations (Rosenzweig, 1950b). Three possible levels of response must be considered in the evaluation of any protocol. There is, first, the *opinion* level, on which the subject gives self-critically censored answers such as he might make in the usual self-report questionnaire. A second level of response is the *overt,* which corresponds to what the person would actually say in a real-life situation. (For general purposes, where contravening information does not exist, it is this overt level that may be assumed to be represented in performance on the P-F Study.) Finally, the subject's answers may reflect the *implicit,* covert, or fantasy level of the personality. It is seldom possible in

---

*A concrete example will clarify this point. If the subject responds to item number 1 on the adult form by writing, "You should not have done that," the examiner actually does not know, without an inquiry, precisely how to score. Without an inquiry he would have to score E since the anonymous figure is presumably administering a reproof; but if in the inquiry, the subject reads back the response by emphatically stressing the word "not," the score E becomes clearly justified. If S does not stress any of the words but instead reads them all in a mild manner, the examiner will ask: "How did the person feel when he said that?" The reply, "He feels sorry that the person didn't do right but doesn't want to blame him," will be scored E;M or possibly even M alone (if the total behavior of S, including facial expression, warrants it). If, on the other hand, S states, "He feels that the person was wrong and is warning him not to make such a mistake again," the score is E. Finally, the score may be M/e if S explains, "Without being angry he is urging the person to be more careful next time." These possible variations are available regardless of the scoring samples since the samples are intended to be used primarily as a general guide where the inquiry has been inconclusive or when there has been no inquiry. Other examples will be found in the P-F manuals.

any projective method to differentiate these levels of response with certainty; the P-F Study shares this common fate. But the inquiry, which is to be conducted at the end of the administration, may often shed light in the given case on this problem. To accomplish this purpose the subject is asked what or whom he was thinking of as he gave his answers, but the question is never directly put as to whether he was thinking of or answering for himself.* Interpretation optimally depends upon the information thus elicited as to set, and the inquiry is therefore strongly recommended, especially if serious research is in question.

Beginning with age nine or ten it is possible to administer the P-F Study to groups when individual administration would be impractical. However, even then subjects should use separate examination blanks, should be allowed to work at their individual speed, and should turn in completed blanks as soon as they are finished; subjects are asked to raise their hands as a signal for the examiner to pick up the leaflets. Total time can then be recorded as in individual administration. Again, if it can be arranged, inquiry should be conducted with each subject as soon as convenient after the group session and before scoring is attempted.

In relation to group administration the question has more than once been raised as to the possibility of presenting the P-F to a large number of subjects at the same time by the use of lantern slides. Though this modification is appealing because of its obvious convenience, both theoretical considerations and the results of our own research, in which such an adaptation has been compared with group administration by booklet, rule it out. One a priori reason is that administration by slides necessitates a uniform time limit on each item for all subjects—too short for some, too long for others—whereas the group method in which each subject has his own booklet permits every individual to proceed at his own rate idiodynamically. Again, the presentation of a stimulus situation to an entire group at the same moment tends to suggest responses in common; for example, if two or three subjects laugh when one of the pictures appears on the screen, this behavior is bound to influence others in the group. But there are also more subtle effects of social facilitation which the instant stimulus in

---

*This point is crucial since, if the inquiry is improperly conducted, it may put the subject on his guard so that he will shift from level three or level two to level one. The examiner must maintain a consistently impartial attitude and convey to S that the inquiry is intended only to clarify what has already been written about (and felt by) the anonymous figure.

common is apt to produce. Administration by slides is therefore incon-sistent with the optimal use of the standard P-F Study and cannot be approved.*

STANDARDIZATION AND OTHER RESEARCH IN BRIEF

Interscorer reliability of the P-F Study has been shown repeatedly to be high (around 85 percent—cf. Clarke, Rosenzweig, and Fleming, 1947). The retest reliability of the instrument has been demonstrated to vary for the several categories and for the GCR, but the correlations are, in general, statistically significant, especially for those categories that relate to direction of aggression (Rosenzweig, Ludwig, and Adel-man, 1975; and see Chapter 2 of the present work). Validity (construct, criterion-related, and pragmatic) has been examined in numerous in-vestigations, mostly with the adult and the children's forms (Nencini and Misiti, 1956b; Pichot and Danjon, 1955). Though investigators vary in their appraisal, the majority of reports are favorable, more so than for most other projective techniques, in part, no doubt, because the P-F is scored more objectively and statistical norms for various ages and for some qualitative conditions are available (Bjerstedt, 1965). The prag-matic relevance of the method has been demonstrated in research on behavior disorders (Davids and Oliver, 1960), psychosomatic condi-tions (Guyotat and Guillaumin, 1960), crime and delinquency (Kaswan, Wasman, and Freedman, 1960; Rauchfleisch, 1973; Rosenzweig, 1963), school adjustment (Roth and Puri, 1967; Spache, 1954), vocational selection (Guion and Gottier, 1965; Van Dam, 1970), and various inter-personal areas (Grygier, 1954). Reviews of investigations of P-F va-lidity have appeared (Rosenzweig, 1960; Rosenzweig and Adelman, 1977).

The adolescent form is the most recent of the three forms; research with it has demonstrated sex differences in aggressive reactions to frustration during the adolescent years (Rosenzweig, 1970a). It is note-worthy in the context of the children's form that, as might hypothe-tically be expected, types and directions of aggression change developmentally from a more impulsive to a more controlled stance (Pareek, 1964; Rosenzweig, 1977a). But, according to other recent findings (Adinolfi, Watson, and Klein, 1973; Saito, 1973), the quality of these changes varies from culture to culture.

---

*Another variation of the standard P-F that has from time to time been suggested is a multiple-choice adaptation to permit rapid and objective scoring. Investigation along these lines, reported in detail in Chapter 3, has led to its rejection.

The P-F has been adapted and standardized worldwide. Parallel to the English (American) version, with separate scoring samples and norms, standardized adaptations are available for one or more of the forms in French, German, Italian, Portuguese, Spanish, Swedish, Hindi, and Japanese.* The applicability of the instrument for cross-cultural research is thus evident, and work along these lines has appeared (see Chapter 4).

---

*The citations for these manuals are as follows: French (Pichot and Danjon, 1956; Pichot, Freson, and Danjon, 1956; Kramer and Le Gat, 1970); German (Hörmann and Moog, 1957; Duhm and Hansen, 1957); Italian (Ferracuti, 1955a, 1955b; Nencini, Banissoni, and Misiti, 1958; Nencini and Belcecchi, 1976); Portuguese (Nick, 1970); Spanish (Cortada de Kohan, 1968); Swedish (Bjerstedt, 1968a, 1968b); Hindi (Pareek, Devi, and Rosenzweig, 1968; Pareek and Rosenzweig, 1959); Japanese (Hayashi and Sumita, 1956, 1957). There are also normative data for large groups of African Congo, Finnish, Sicilian, and Dutch children that are not cited here because these data were not gathered under authorized conditions and are not therefore comparable to the norms obtained with the parallel versions.

2   Test-Retest Reliability

The reliability of projective techniques has been one of the most baffling issues in the field of psychological measurement. The root of the problem lies in the usual insistence on employing criteria of reliability appropriate to psychometric tests, especially the assumption of item homogeneity. Such criteria make no allowance for the fact that in projective methods a subject is often intentionally presented with a variety of stimulus items on the assumption that an idiodynamic pattern of responses will be elicited (Rosenzweig, 1951a). In addition, it is from "the configuration of the entire succession of item responses" (Rosenzweig, 1960, p. 162) that projective techniques aim to determine crucial characteristics of the person. Reliability measures which assume internal and linear consistency or which compare the first and second halves or odd-even items as equivalents therefore violate the basic nature of projective, or even of semiprojective, devices, the latter of which are exemplified by the P-F Study.

Guilford (1950, p. 484) lends support to this rationale. In the American Psychological Association (APA) *Standards for Educational and Psychological Tests and Manuals (1966),* the problem is broached as follows: "The recommendations herein presented are necessarily of a psychometric nature and should not be interpreted as necessarily applying to all users of projective techniques" (p. 4). But inasmuch as idiodynamic interpretation is dependent upon at least partial use of demographic norms, psychometric criteria should be applied to such techniques, albeit with qualifications.

This chapter is intended as a survey of research dealing with the reliability of the Rosenzweig P-F Study. Analysis of variance, split-half, and retest procedures are reviewed and their relative effectiveness evaluated. In this context, reliability measures as applied to projective techniques in general will be discussed.

SCORING SCHEMA

The rubrics used for scoring the responses on the P-F have been described in Chapter 1 (see Table 1), but it will be useful for the following exposition to highlight the scoring schema under its six categories and nine factors. (See Table 2.) It should be observed that the factors alone serve for the actual scores assigned by the examiner; the scoring blank provides for recomposing the factors into the six categories. But these latter are the basic constructs of the Study and are regarded as more essential than the factors for protocol interpretation and for assessing reliability and validity.

It is crucial to note that the constructs of the P-F do not involve types (or traits) of personality. Instead types of reaction or behavior, available to everyone, are posited. The responses elicited by the P-F are treated as a sample of the characteristic (not necessarily permanent or constant) reaction types of the subject.

THE PROBLEM OF RELIABILITY

Several investigators of the reliability of the P-F Study have concentrated on the internal consistency of its scoring variables. Taylor (1952) and Taylor and Taylor (1951) evaluated the consistency of the P-F scoring categories and the GCR by analysis of variance methods. They reported little reliability for the GCR and a range of reliability for the

TABLE 2: Types and Directions of Aggression (Six Categories Combined in Nine Factors)

TYPES ➞	Obstacle-Dominance (O-D)	Ego-Defense (E-D)	Need-Persistence (N-P)
DIRECTIONS ↓	FACTORS		
Extraggression (E-A)	Extrapeditive (E)	Extrapunitive (E)	Extrapersistive (e)
Intraggression (I-A)	Intropeditive (I)	Intropunitive (I)	Intropersistive (i)
Imaggression (M-A)	Impeditive (M)	Impunitive (M)	Impersistive (m)

scoring categories of from .58 to .10. They attributed the low reliability to large item variance and, therefore, low internal consistency. Sutcliffe (1955), who employed item analysis and intercorrelation, states that "the P-F Study is unsatisfactory as a measuring instrument" (p. 106). This conclusion is drawn from data purporting to show that item homogeneity and trait generality are not found in the P-F. A later criticism appeared in *Measuring Human Behavior (Lake, Miles, and Earle, 1973)*. From a split-half measure (odd-even items), the authors reported that P-F reliabilities were poor for direction of aggression and virtually nonexistent for type of aggression. In point of fact, their own data show the correlations for all three directions of aggression significant at the .01 level (except for I-A, which reached .01 significance in one group and .05 significance in another group); for type of aggression the correlations for N-P in one group and O-D in another group were significant at the .05 level.

Rosenzweig (1956a) has taken both Sutcliffe and Taylor and Taylor to task for overlooking the largely projective nature of the P-F Study. He has pointed out that heterogeneity of variables is fostered by this device to tap unique interrelationships of personality. The P-F Study and other semiprojective techniques are structured in such a way as to produce an inherently large item variance. In this light the values for internal consistency found by Taylor (1952) are surprisingly high. In fact, it is only the inclusion of GCR situations that allows the P-F to show reliability when measured by methods which demand low item variance (Taylor, 1952, p. 152) as crucial to reliability. GCR items tend to elicit a stereotyped response and are thus most like psychometric test items. They are largely responsible for the internal consistency which the P-F does demonstrate.

The conventional method of measuring reliability by the split-half procedure is often inappropriate for projective instruments since it can seldom be assumed that responses to the two halves of the test are equivalent; indeed, in methods like the Rorschach, where the sequence of items is an important variable, interpretation of the protocol rests heavily on the contrary assumption that all responses do not have equivalent significance for the individual. The disparity in mean scores of responses to the odd and even items of the P-F, as well as the absence of consistently high correlation between the two halves, shows that, unlike the usual intelligence or attitude scale, the various situations of the Study do not have equivalent significance for the subject, but, by their very design, tend to elicit different sorts of response. This lack of equivalence among the items is inherent in the construction of the P-F.

It would, of course, be possible to construct a scale similar to the P-F in which all the items were of equal stimulus value for the subject;

such a procedure is conceivable even for more complicated methods such as the TAT and the Rorschach (see *Hill, 1972; Holtzman, Thorpe, Swartz, and Herron, 1961*). But the limitations of such a course are obvious. The Holtzman Ink Blot Test, intended as an improvement over the Rorschach with respect to psychometric criteria, has been found to have some highly significant split-half reliability correlations, but item homogeneity has even in this technique been ruled out from the outset.

RELIABILITY OF THE ADULT FORM

The investigation described here was carried out some 20 years ago and was alluded to by Mirmow (1952b) when she summarized unpublished projects of the P-F Study done at our laboratory. However, because the data have intrinsic interest and importance to the whole issue of reliability, they are now presented in detail.

Subjects and Procedure

Two separate groups of normal subjects were employed. The first consisted of 35 female student nurses, ranging in age from 19 to 25 years (mean age, 20.4 years); the second included 45 male medical-school freshmen, 18 to 38 years of age (mean, 22.8 years).

The P-F was administered twice to each group, first under ordinary conditions, and again with instructions to respond as spontaneously as possible without conscious intent to duplicate previous responses. The interval between the first and second testing was two months in the case of the student nurses, and seven and one-half months for the medical freshmen. Differences between the results for these two groups may therefore be attributable to sex differences and/or to the influence of the variable time interval. Responses to both examinations were scored in terms of the six P-F scoring categories and the GCR. At the time of this research, the GCR items were 12 in number. On the basis of a larger normative population, the GCR items later became 16 in number (Rosenzweig, 1967b). However, the difference between the original and the revised GCR has been shown to be insignificant in its effect on research data. "The revision of the criteria for the GCR need not invalidate the conclusions of previous investigations employing the former standards" (Rosenzweig, 1967b, p. 60).

Results: Comparison of Odd and Even Items on Test 1

Mean Results. The split-half reliability of the P-F was determined by comparing the results of odd- with even-numbered items on test 1.

Means and standard deviations of odd and even items for all categories are presented for the male and female subjects in Table 3. Inspection of the results for the male subjects shows the two groups of items to be clearly unequal with respect to direction of aggression. Mean E-A percent for the odd items is seen to be 53.1 in contrast to 39.8 for the even-numbered situations. This difference has a t value of 6.33 ($p<.01$). Significant differences are also found for I-A percent ($t = 2.28$, $p < .05$) and for M-A percent ($t = 8.50$, $p < .01$), while mean percentages for type of aggression are essentially undifferentiated for the odd and even items.

For the female group, significant differences between the mean results for the odd and even items are found in four of the six scoring categories. The even items are significantly lower in E-A percent ($t = 4.08$, $p < .01$) and E-D percent ($t = 4.61$, $p < .01$), and higher in M-A percent ($t = 4.82$, $p < .01$) and O-D percent ($t = 2.38$, $p < .05$). Differences in I-A percent and N-P percent are not statistically significant.

Therefore, it is apparent that for both groups of subjects, the odd and even items of the P-F Study are of unequal weight in eliciting the various categorized responses to frustration. This inequality is particu-

TABLE 3: Means, Standard Deviations, and Product-Moment Correlations of P-F Categories for Odd versus Even Items

Category	E-A Percent	I-A Percent	M-A Percent	O-D Percent	E-D Percent	N-P Percent
Males ($N = 45$)						
Odd items						
Mean	53.1	27.7	19.2	17.5	50.5	31.9
Standard deviation	13.5	10.9	7.4	9.4	12.6	11.2
Even items						
Mean	39.8	22.8	37.3	16.6	50.1	33.2
Standard deviation	16.1	10.9	12.4	8.3	16.8	14.9
Females ($N = 35$)						
Odd items						
Mean	52.5	27.9	19.6	20.9	56.6	22.4
Standard deviation	13.9	9.7	9.0	11.0	11.7	11.2
Even items						
Mean	39.6	28.8	31.6	25.5	47.1	27.5
Standard deviation	15.2	10.0	12.8	12.6	13.3	12.4
Males r correlation	+.57*	+.15	+.06	+.21	+.41*	+.46*
Females r correlation	+.21	−.47*	+.16	+.56*	+.55*	−.04

*$p < .01$.

larly striking with respect to direction of aggression, in which the odd items, in both males and females, tend to evoke more extraggressive responses, while the even items elicit more imaggressive ones.

Correlation Results. Pearson product-moment correlations between odd and even items, corrected for attenuation by the Spearman-Brown prophecy formula, are presented for both groups of subjects in Table 3. For the male subjects, significant positive association is found only in E-A percent, E-D percent, and N-P percent, while correlations for other categories are negligible. In the female subjects, significant positive relationship appears only for O-D percent and E-D percent. Correlations for E-A percent, M-A percent, and N-P percent are low, while I-A percent shows significant negative correspondence between the odd and even items. The various scoring categories of the P-F Study thus only selectively show significant reliability as determined by the split-half method.

Comparison of Initial and Retest Administrations

Mean Results. Means and standard deviations on test 1 and 2 for the six P-F scoring categories and for the GCR are presented for the male and female groups in Table 4. No mean difference between the two tests greater than two percentage points appears in either group for any of the variables measured. Moreover, none of these discrepancies, as measured by the formula for computing the significance of the difference between correlated means, proved to be statistically significant. It is therefore concluded that the mean results for the major scoring dimensions of the P-F are essentially comparable in the two administrations.

Correlation Results. Test-retest correlations for the P-F categories and the GCR in the two groups are also presented in Table 4. All variables in the male group are significant—E-A, M-A, E-D, N-P, and GCR at the .01 level, and I-A and O-D at the .05 level; among the females, all correlations are significant at the .01 level, except the O-D, which is significant at the .05 level, and GCR, which does not reach significance.

With regard to direction of aggression, the highest degree of reliability is found for extraggression, where correlations of +.56 and +.61 ($p < .01$) are found for males and females, respectively. Correlations for imaggression also indicate a relatively high level of reliability (+.51 for males; +.59 for females; both significant at $p < .01$). Figures for intraggression are significant in both groups—+.35 in the male group ($p < .05$), and +.44 in the female group ($p < .01$)—even though the actual correlations are comparatively low.

Among scores for type of aggression, both need-persistence and ego-defense show good consistency in the two tests; that is, significance for both categories in both groups reaches the .01 level. Obstacle-dominance is significant for both groups at the .05 level, but it shows less consistency in the two tests than do the other types of aggression (O-D = +.34 in both groups).

The GCR, although highly reliable among the male subjects (r = .58, $p < .01$), is found to have a retest correlation of only +.21 in the female group, with only a slight, and nonsignificant, relationship in the two tests.

When the results for the male and female groups are compared, no consistent differences are apparent. Correlations for categories dealing with direction of aggression tend to be higher for the female subjects, whereas those for type of aggression and GCR are higher for the males. However, significant relationships for all variables are evident for both groups, with the exception of the GCR, in which significant reliability

TABLE 4: Means, Standard Deviations, and Retest Correlations of P-F Scoring Categories and GCR on Tests 1 and 2

Category	E-A Percent	I-A Percent	M-A Percent	O-D Percent	E-D Percent	N-P Percent	GCR Percent
Males (N=45)							
Test 1							
Mean	46.5	25.2	28.2	17.0	50.5	32.6	69.4
Standard deviation	12.31	8.07	7.25	6.58	11.70	10.50	13.02
Test 2							
Mean	46.1	26.0	27.9	18.7	48.7	32.6	71.7
Standard deviation	12.59	6.77	9.12	7.92	9.59	10.62	13.05
Females (N=35)							
Test 1							
Mean	46.7	28.2	25.0	22.4	48.4	29.3	67.1
Standard deviation	10.73	7.08	9.41	5.75	8.54	8.48	15.60
Test 2							
Mean	46.9	28.5	24.6	20.9	47.8	31.5	67.6
Standard deviation	14.13	7.98	11.07	7.51	9.72	9.94	13.23
Males (all)							
r correlation	+.56**	+.35*	+.51**	+.34*	+.61**	+.71**	+.58**
Females (all)							
r correlation	+.61**	+.44**	+.59**	+.34*	+.46**	+.47**	+.21

*$p < .05$.
**$p < .01$.

is found only for the males. Whether this discrepancy may be ascribed to a sex difference in the consistency of the GCR, whether it represents a function of the varying length of the interval between tests in the two groups, or whether it is attributable merely to the operation of uncontrolled conditions in the selection of the two groups, cannot be determined from the present data.

When test-retest coefficients of reliability for the various categories are compared with those yielded by the split-half technique, it is clear that the former method demonstrates higher reliability. Whereas the retest correlations show significant correspondence for all of the categories in both males and females, the odd-even coefficients are statistically significant in only 50 percent of the scores and show little consistency in the two groups of subjects. These results, together with the finding that mean scores of the first and retest administrations of the P-F are more comparable than those of the two halves of the Study, appear to demonstrate the greater appropriateness of the test-retest method.

As part of the original treatment of the data an additional computation was included at this point. The percentage of change in GCR versus non-GCR situations from one administration to the next was calculated. This analysis was accomplished by weighting changes of response and then dividing the number of responses in which changes occurred by the total number of responses to each kind of item. GCR items were found to show significantly less change in direction of aggression in both groups of subjects than non-GCR items. With respect to type of aggression, however, GCR items produced greater stability than other items only among the male subjects. From these results it was concluded that, as might be anticipated, retest reliability is, in general, greater for stimulus situations to which a model group-response is given.

Other Investigations of Retest Reliability

The retest reliability of the adult form of the P-F Study has been investigated by other psychologists. Bernard (1949), working with 105 adults who were retested after an average interval of four months, reported consistency coefficients as follows: E-A = .73; I-A = .52; M-A = .69; O-D = .58; E-D = .73; N-P = .71; GCR = .45. He also analyzed the same data to determine item reliability and found consistency values which, for the 24 items, ranged from .51 to .79, with a mean of .61. In his judgment, these figures for item reliability are "satisfactory. "

Pichot and Danjon (1955) retested a group of 59 psychology students, 32 females and 27 males, after four months and found correlations as follows: E-A = .64; I-A = .34; M-A = .68; OD = .46; E-D = .68; N-P = .57; GCR = .58. (Neither Bernard nor Pichot and Danjon indicate levels of significance for their correlations.) Sanford and Rosenstock (1952) retested single items after an interval of one month and obtained repeat reliabilities of .54 and .57 for two pictures based upon rank-difference coefficients. They concluded that a test composed of items having a consistency as good as these would be a reliable instrument.

These findings corroborate the results from our laboratory in that the retest reliability coefficients are of the same order as those we obtained. In view of the inappropriateness of applying most psychometric criteria of reliability to projective techniques, coefficients of this magnitude suffice to demonstrate the retest reliability of the adult form of the P-F Study.

RETEST RELIABILITY OF THE ADOLESCENT FORM

A group of 16 high school students, nine females and seven males, aged 17–18, were given a second P-F one month after an initial administration.

The following retest correlations were obtained: E-A = .79; I-A = .86; M-A = .67; O-D = .30; E-D = .43; N-P = .52; GCR = .62. Correlations for all directions of aggression and GCR were significant at the .01 level. Need-persistence was significant at the .05 level but O-D and E-D did not reach significance. These results are in keeping with findings for the adult form. Correlations for directions of aggression tend to be more reliable than those for types of aggression.

RETEST RELIABILITY OF THE CHILDREN'S FORM

In a project involving a group of elementary school children, the subjects were 45 children, nine to 13 years of age, who were retested after ten months. Retest correlations were E-A = .44; I-A = .25; M-A = .50; O-D = .18; E-D = .55; N-P = .49; GCR = .22. The results for E-A, M-A, E-D, and N-P were significant at the .01 level; the others did not reach significance (compare Rosenzweig, 1960).

Pareek (1958a, 1964), in an investigation of 50 12-year-old boys, used the Indian adaptation of the children's form of the P-F with an interval of two and one-half months between test and retest. His retest correlations were E-A = .75; I-A = .62; M-A = .71; O-D = .62; E-D = .78; N-P = .72; GCR = .56. (He reports no significance levels.)

It is also noteworthy that this same investigator carried out an analysis of retest-item reliability with the group of subjects described above. He reports coefficients of consistency for the 24 items that range from .56 to .91, with a mean of .70.

Given the problems involved in determining the reliability of semiprojective tests, the children's form of the P-F Study has been shown to be as reliable as could be expected. These results tend to support the conclusion from the previous findings for the adult and adolescent forms that retest coefficients are more appropriate for demonstrating the reliability of the P-F Study than is the split-half method.

CONCLUSION

The dynamic investigation of personality involves observation of the individual in a variety of situations in an attempt to evaluate the flexibility of his adjustment to changing stimuli with varying emotional connotations. (See *Mischel, 1968*.) Lack of equivalence among the items of projective instruments is an inevitable consequence of the rationale of these methods, which precludes strict adherence to some of the conventional criteria of test reliability, namely, internal consistency.

The alternative statistical approach to reliability—correlations of test results obtained from the same group of subjects on separate occasions—presents other difficulties for the projective methods. Although the test-retest method has a distinct advantage over the split-half technique, since the configurational qualities of the total instrument are preserved, obstacles are still encountered. Unlike such relatively static capacities as intelligence, for example, personality characteristics are assumed to be more-or-less highly modifiable by environmental events, and hence may show fluctuation from first to second testing, without necessarily reflecting doubt upon the validity of the initial results. A more serious problem lies in the impossibility of duplicating, in a retest situation, the conditions under which the projective technique was initially administered. The approach of the subject to the unstructured stimuli of the instrument may be altered, to an unknown extent, by the mere circumstance of his having already seen and responded to the material. And, finally, the use of correlational methods for determining the retest reliability of a projective instrument involves all the inadequacies attendant upon the segmental treatment of essentially configurational data.

These limitations notwithstanding, the retest approach is still the best one available for determining the reliability of projective techniques. But to expect such techniques to achieve reliability coefficients as high as those found for some psychometric tests is unrealistic. In the last analysis, it is the validity of a test that must be paramount; reliability as such is valueless and has at times been mistakenly valued above validity. Adapting an ancient philosophical dictum, one might say that reliability without validity is empty; validity without reliability is dubious. (In support of this general position, see *Cronbach, 1970*.)

With specific reference to the P-F Study, the foregoing survey demonstrates a comparatively high degree of retest reliability for the adult, adolescent, and children's forms. It has also been shown that internal consistency and split-half methods are not as apposite as retest correlation for ascertaining the assessment consistency of the P-F and similar semiprojective techniques.

3   Construct Validity

The reliability and validity of projective and semiprojective techniques cannot be truly determined if one is bound by the constraints appropriate to psychometric tests. This position was advanced by Rosenzweig (1951a, 1956a) and further explored in a later paper regarding the reliability of the Rosenzweig P-F Study (Rosenzweig, Ludwig, and Adelman, 1975). In the *APA Standards for Educational and Psychological Tests and Manuals (1966,* p. 4) it is argued that projective techniques often produce data which are more qualitative than quantitative and therefore require more flexible and less psychometrically bound means of evaluation than are required by other tests. This chapter develops this tenet in respect to validity. At the outset a framework is presented, as derived from APA standards, with which the validity of semiprojective techniques in general can be explored. Then, within this frame, the construct validity of the P-F Study is examined.

THE PROBLEM OF VALIDITY

The initial task in assessing the validity of any measuring device involves the selection of appropriate evaluative criteria. The selection process must be grounded in a thorough understanding of the concepts which underlie the technique and delimit the particular contexts— whether these involve reaction to experimental manipulation, differentiation of nosological groups, or predictions of situational behavior—in which the technique is applied (Rosenzweig, 1951a; *Blatt, 1975*). With all clinical instruments, validation must be approached by integrating many sources of evidence since no single criterion measure is ever sufficient *(Macfarlane, 1942).*

Projective methods are not unidimensional, univocal *tests,* but are usually multidimensional and flexible *tools* or instruments. The validity of any such method

> depends upon the skill and experience of the clinician who employs it; the only relevant question bearing on validity that can be asked from this standpoint is whether, by virtue of its design, it facilitates the skill of the clinical psychologist in achieving those insights which he is striving to acquire (Rosenzweig, 1959).

Cronbach (1971) lends support to this position in stating that "one validates, not a test, but an interpretation of data arising from a specified procedure" (p. 447).

Since the inherent flexibility of projective instruments allows subjects to respond selectively to diverse features of the technique according to their problems, needs, and interests, the validity of such instruments depends upon the degree to which such variable expression is facilitated. The subject's use of the technique defines the dimensions of validity. An important consideration is the level or levels of behavior elicited by the instrument: the clinician must decide whether the subject's test behavior is based on socially derived opinions; everyday, overt behavior; or implicit (unconscious or latent) attitudes; or some combination of the three (Rosenzweig, 1950b). This distinction is paramount whenever attempts are made to evaluate, match, or predict specific behaviors. It follows that the validity of any semiprojective instrument will be partially defined by psychometric criteria but greatly affected by the interpretive ability of the clinician. These instruments, therefore, never have univocal validity; they have variable validity vis-a-vis the total interaction of subject, situation, and examiner *(Blatt, 1975).*

Nevertheless, the approximate optimal validity of a semiprojective device can be estimated and reported, and it is important to do so since a device which, employed by various examiners in varying situations, fails to demonstrate measurable validity is adding nothing to the interpersonal skills of the examiner and would accordingly be useless. It is with this assumption in mind that the validity of projective and semiprojective techniques has to be approached.

VALIDATION SCHEMA

Three aspects of validity may be differentiated: construct validity and criterion-related validity—both primary aspects; and pragmatic validity—a secondary aspect.

Construct validity is determined by the degree to which explanatory concepts (or constructs) account for test performance. Included under this head are investigations in which there has been experimental examination or manipulation of variables directly related to the constructs on which the instrument depends, with subsequent comparison between hypothesized and actual results. Attempts to determine the level of behavior elicited by the technique are essential. Also included are direct comparisons between the instrument and other devices which purport to measure the same or similar constructs. However, the scope of construct validity should not be exaggerated, as has been done by some authors *(Messick, 1975).*

Criterion-related validity is determined by the degree to which scores correlate with external variables which provide an independent measure of the behavior in question. Included under criterion-related validity are investigations in which the primary aim has been to find correlations between technique scores and criterion measures not directly related to constructs, for example, correlation of P-F scores with those of the Allport-Vernon Study of Values. Attempts to make predictive use of a technique or to correlate observer ratings with technique scores also belong in this category. One such approach which has been used with the P-F is that of successive clinical predictions (Rosenzweig, 1950c). A number of investigators in conference attempt to predict, on the basis of case-history and other test data, the responses of a given subject to the projective instrument. Finally, criterion-related validity examines the sensitivity of the instrument to the external criteria which conceptually differentiate between two or more subject groups.

Pragmatic validity is newly defined here as validity only indirectly related to the constructs on which the instrument is based but with practical relevance derived from attempts to apply the instrument for purposes of selection or screening in one or another social setting. Because the technique and its constructs are not the focus of investigation, the results of such research can have only a secondary bearing on validity. However, positive results may point the direction for further primary exploration of construct or criterion-related validity, and negative findings may help delimit the areas of useful application of a technique.

With the above orientation, part of what has been called "content validity" may be incorporated in pragmatic validity. Through extended use of a technique one can determine how well the test content "samples ... the class of situations or subject matter about which conclusions are to be drawn" *(American Psychological Association, 1966,* p. 12). In projective and semiprojective techniques, however, content validity as such has limited relevance since it is in the nature of these tools to provide unstructured situations to which the individual can impart meaning on the basis of his own experiential orientation.

The rest of this chapter is limited to a single aspect of the validity paradigm, namely, construct validity, with special reference to the P-F Study. In view of the fact that the P-F is a hypothetico-deductive instrument, built on constructs of frustration theory, it must, above all other considerations, possess the validity of these constructs. Since considerable work concerning the validity of the children's form has already been reviewed (Rosenzweig, 1960) and data for the adolescent form are as yet sketchy (due to its relatively recent development), the emphasis of the present chapter will be on the adult form. Investigations involving the children's form will, however, be included when they decisively contribute to the understanding of basic P-F constructs. Unless otherwise specified, all reported P-F investigations in this discussion employed the adult form.

EVOLUTION OF P-F CONSTRUCTS

The Rosenzweig P-F Study grew out of a research program designed to validate the concepts of psychoanalysis by experimental methods. Laboratory investigations of repression, displacement, and projection threw into relief the phenomena of frustration as best epitomizing the psychodynamic approach in its experimental implications (Rosenzweig and Mason, 1934; Rosenzweig, 1938c, 1941). A heuristic classification of directions of aggression in reaction to frustration (extrapunitive, intropunitive, impunitive) was formulated (Rosenzweig, 1934b), geared to a behavioral research methodology involving selective reaction to successfully completed versus uncompleted tasks (Rosenzweig, 1935). Children who were rated high for the trait of pride tended to recall finished tasks more often than unfinished ones while children rated low showed the opposite recall behavior (Rosenzweig and Mason, 1934). This basic methodology was refined through more stringent experimental control and employed in a research program on repression, with special reference to ego-defense vis-à-vis need-persistence, a distinction which later provided two of the chief P-F scoring rubrics (Rosenzweig, 1943). Adult (college) subjects were administered puzzles (half of which they were allowed to complete and half of which were interrupted before completion) under formal and informal conditions. Subjects in formal conditions (intelligence test) later recalled more of their successes than failures while those who performed under informal conditions (to help in classifying the puzzles as to difficulty) later recalled more unfinished puzzles than finished ones. The full mechanism of repression was thus found to involve not only the ego-defensive forgetting of the unpleasant but the need-persistive retention of the unfinished. An early exploratory experiment with preschool children (aged three to five) was performed by Heller (1939). In this work, the modes of reaction to frustration demonstrating need-persistence and ego-defense, with the extrapunitive, intropunitive, and impunitive dimensions of the latter construct, were systematically observed and qualitatively defined. At this time Burnham (1939) by work with 45 adolescent subjects confirmed that the responses to the semiprojective P-F agreed more closely with overt behavior than with opinion behavior (self-ratings) in placing blame after failure. In addition, this research showed that individuals tended to behave more extrapunitively in tasks on which they considered themselves to have good ability, more intropunitively or impunitively in those for which their self-estimates of ability were low. From all this research on the clinically derived concepts of psychoanalysis there emerged an experimentally based outline of frustration theory (Rosenzweig, 1944).*

In the same year in which the heuristic classification of directions of aggression was first presented there also appeared a suggestion for making personality tests more valid (Rosenzweig, 1934a). It was hypothesized that by devising questions to tap two different levels of response (actual and ideal), corrective factors for personality inventories could be obtained. This idea, which grew up side by side with the research in experimental psychodynamics and which pointed the way for an experimental examination of projective constructs, was incorporated along with frustration theory in the design of the P-F Study. The P-F allows the subject to project himself into the stimulus situation and identify with the central, frustrated figure and at the same time provides for both a meaningful and measurable categorization of responses. What has become conceptually explicit in P-F research is the varying extent to which such projection takes place and can be experimentally manipulated with diverse effects on level of psychodiagnostic behavior (Rosenzweig, 1950b).

The evidence for the validity of the P-F Study is derived, first, from developmental research which demonstrates consistently different modes of reaction to P-F stimuli as the age of subjects advances. Next, the self-consistent conceptual patterns discovered in basic research on reaction to frustration will be considered (for example, the triadic hy-

---

*An epitome of the research in experimental psychodynamics that produced the basic constructs (scoring categories and factors) of the P-F Study will be found in Chapter 5. The hypothetico-deductive nature of the instrument is evident from this review of its history and provides a large part of its inherent construct validity.

pothesis). The manner in which the P-F is situationally experienced by the individual subject concomitant with the level of response is then explored, and evidence presented for the generalizability of verbal aggression on the P-F to other measures of opinion, overt, and implicit behavior. Investigations involving the effect upon P-F scores of the experimental induction of frustration demonstrate the interaction of situational and personality variables. Finally the physiological correlates of the P-F aggression categories will be examined.

Developmental Evidence

Psychodynamic theory asserts that outwardly expressed aggression (hostility) is developmentally a more primitive form than either inwardly turned or turned-off aggression. The evolution of an individual's repertoire of aggressive behaviors is assumed to follow a progression mirroring the socialization process; that is, in the course of growth the child learns to inhibit hostile reactions to frustration and acquires patterns of social conformity and personal responsibility. P-F Study constructs imply such a developmental sequence and this sequence is supported by the normative data of the P-F.

The children's form was originally standardized with a group of 256 children aged four to 13 (Rosenzweig, Fleming, and Rosenzweig, 1948). Results show that during childhood there is a steady decrease in frequency of extraggression from age four (56.4 percent) to 13 (40.5 percent). In the same time period intraggression and imaggression rise from 19.9 percent to 29.5 percent and from 23.7 percent to 30.4 percent, respectively, while the GCR (a measure of social adjustment) rises from 52.1 percent to 63.8 percent (all comparisons significant at $p < .01$). Zimet, Rose, and Camp (1973) found a similar shift away from E-A and toward I-A with increasing age. A rise in need-persistence with increasing age appeared in normative data and was supported by Stoltz and Smith (1959), who found that with growing maturity children come to expect more solutions to problems. In addition to these American data there are norms based on large groups of French, Italian, German, Swedish, Japanese, and Indian children (see Rosenzweig, 1960). Pareek (1964) compared findings for his Indian standardization of the P-F (based on 1,002 subjects) with those for the Japanese and American normative groups. Significant developmental similarities appeared across all groups: E-A steadily decreased while I-A, M-A, and GCR increased from age four to 13—despite the fact that cultural differences, reflecting diverse patterns of socialization, could be discerned. For example, Japanese children showed a greater I-A percent at age eight than American or Indian children, while at age 13 Americans showed the highest I-A percent. The most striking aspect of cross-cultural investigations, however, is the uniformity of the overall developmental progression.

During adolescence there is a predictable rise in extraggression and ego (etho)-defense and a fall in intraggression and group conformity as the teenager goes through a period of identity seeking and rebellion against authority (Rosenzweig and Braun, 1970; Rosenzweig, 1970a). This pattern is most visible in males, but females show nonsignificant tendencies in the same directions. As the teens draw to a close, these P-F scores for both sexes revert to 13-year-old levels. Girls, in contrast to boys, show a significant increase in need-persistence from early to late adolescence, in accordance with the recognized fact that girls mature physically and psychologically faster than boys and are able to find alternative outlets for their hostile aggression sooner than boys are. However, further evidence for these preliminary findings with adolescents is needed.

As young adulthood begins there is a stabilization in all scoring categories, which is maintained through middle age (Rosenzweig, 1950d). Adults 50 to 80 years old show a significant increase in E-A ($p < .05$) and E-D ($p < .05$) and a decrease in M-A ($p < .05$) and GCR ($p < .01$). These changes may be viewed as indicating a trend toward senility when some individuals become set in their ways, less willing to compromise, and prone to defend themselves by attacking others. It must be noted, however, that these conclusions are drawn from a very small sample of older adult subjects (Rosenzweig, 1952). There is need for further research to enrich the norms for this senior population.

Biochemical knowledge on maturation is congruent with the foregoing developmental behavior findings. At birth the adrenal medulla consists largely of norepinephrine but with development epinephrine levels increase *(Hokfelt, 1951).* Work with psychotics tends to indicate that a parallel reversal in the physiological states of development accompanies psychological regression: "Thus, paranoid patients, whose illness is [psychoanalytically assumed to be] characteristic of an earlier stage of development than that of depressed patients, show a physiology characteristic of an earlier phase of development [excessive norepinephrine secretion] than that shown by depressed patients [excessive epinephrine secretion]" (Funkenstein, King, and Drolette, 1957, p. 171).

Both the behavioral norms established for the P-F and cognate research regarding physiological development corroborate the theoretical assumptions which underlie the P-F Study and thus afford evidence for its construct validity.

Self-Consistent Conceptual Patterns

Another approach to determining construct validity is by exploring the extent to which scoring variables form self-consistent patterns which have interpretive significance in terms of underlying theory. In an investigation in which reaction times for emitting E-A responses were found to be shorter than those of I-A or M-A, Fritz (reported by Mirmow, 1952b) was able to support the hypothesis that E-A is the most immediate and least inhibited direction of aggression. Parsons (1955) discovered that E-A scores correlated negatively with test duration ($p < .05$) while N-P and I-A scores correlated positively ($p < .01$).

Rosenzweig (1952) investigated the relationship between number of words used in responses to P-F stimulus situations and the scores of these responses. He employed a group of 73 normal subjects. Results for direction of aggression showed a consistent tendency for M-A responses to be significantly shorter ($p < .01$) than E-A or I-A responses. (The conciliatory M-A responses may consume less time because a decision regarding the direction of aggression is avoided.) There was a related result for types of aggression. The O-D response, with blocking in the face of frustration, proved to be the shortest in word count, while E-D and N-P responses, perhaps representing stages of advance toward a constructive solution, were progressively longer.

The idiodynamic nature of the P-F as a semiprojective technique is in part disclosed through the analysis of Trends, that is, changes in response scores during the course of the examination. These modes of responding to one's own responses have been classified as response-dominance (R→R) in contrast to stimulus-dominance (S→R), which is characteristic of psychometric tests (Rosenzweig, 1951a). Trends have been found to appear in conjunction with such other indicators of low frustration tolerance as decreased extraggression and ego (etho)-defense and increased intraggression, imaggression, and obstacle-dominance (Rosenzweig, 1952). But in this same preliminary study trends were not found to be diagnostically reliable in distinguishing between groups of psychiatric patients. It should be recalled, however, that the P-F Study is not expected to serve for such diagnostic purposes and, more particularly, that the essential concept of trends is idiodynamic, not demographic, in intent. The validity of trends is hence not seriously impugned by this finding.

An intensive investigation of the validity of trends conducted on the entire original standardization sample of the children's form deserves special attention (Rosenzweig and Mirmow, 1950). A developmental analysis disclosed that after age five a sharp increase in the number of trends appeared—a result interpreted as reflecting the process of socialization at the actual fifth year with an attendant suppression of infantile aggression and a concomitant arousal of conflict in reaction to frustration. Subjects with trends showed significantly lower E, higher I, and higher O-D scores than those without any trends, a result taken to indicate that trends reflect the inhibition of external hostility, and increase of guilt and of blocking (conflict).

A scarcity of such trends was found in teenage problem children and was interpreted as an indication of immaturity and undersocialization (Rosenzweig and Rosenzweig, 1952). An abundance of immature trends at age level 10–12 in that investigation was found to be associated with estimates of social inadequacy. But while there is some evidence that a notable prominence of trends in an individual case is an indication of personal instability and low frustration tolerance, the basis is tentative. In any event, adequate idiodynamic interpretation of trends requires recognition of the types of trends present, the corresponding category and GCR scores, as well as the chronological maturity of the subject. There is a compelling need for further research in this area, the results of which are potentially very important.

A theoretical pattern involving reaction to frustration as related to the psychoanalytic mechanisms of defense and susceptibility to suggestion was illuminated through experimental research on repression and hypnosis. The long history of research associating hysteria with hypnosis, and Freudian formulations of psychodynamics linking hysteria with repression, implied a relationship between repression and hypnotizability. Thus there implicitly evolved

> a *triadic hypothesis* according to which hypnotizability as a personality trait is to be found in positive association with repression as a preferred mechanism of defense and with impunitiveness as a characteristic type of immediate reaction to frustration. Non-hypnotizability would, by implication, be linked with other defense mechanisms, e.g., displacement and projection, and with other types of reaction to frustration, e.g., intropunitiveness and extrapunitiveness (Rosenzweig, 1938c, p. 489).

Each triadic component, however, was also assumed to have other peculiar characteristics, and intercorrelations of the components would therefore be less than perfect.

A number of investigations have substantiated the triadic hypothesis. With three groups of college students, Rosenzweig and Sarason (1942) obtained scores for directions of aggression on the P-F, measures of liability to the repression of unpleasant experiences, and ratings of hypnotizability or suggestibility. The correlations between M-A and repression were .19, .39, and .54, while correlations between E-A and repression were −.30, −.73, and −.26. (I-A relationships were inconsistent.) Imaggression also correlated highly with suggestibility/hypnotizability: .57, .47, .78. The correlations between suggestibility and repression were .25 and .47, and between hypnotizability and repression .66. Multiple correlation coefficients above .75 were found for each of the three components, with the correlation of hypnotizability with repression and imaggression being the highest (.83).

A significant relationship between degree of suggestibility and direction of aggression was found by Kates (1951). Children who scored low on a test of suggestibility had significantly higher E-A scores than children who scored high on the test; suggestible children had significantly higher M-A scores than nonsuggestible children. Research on the triadic hypothesis has also been extended to clinical populations (Canter, 1953). Psycholeptic patients (having hysterical character disorders) obtained significantly higher repression scores and lower E-A scores than epileptic patients (with idiopathic epilepsy). The hysterical group also showed a tendency toward higher M-A scores although no significant differences in hypnotizability were found. The triadic hypothesis tends to be supported by this research.

Under other rubrics a revival of interest in the relationships between direction of aggression and defense mechanisms has appeared as the "repressor-sensitizer" dichotomy (Altrocchi, Shrauger, and McLeod, 1964). This dichotomy has been further expanded to include "expressors." With this extension the formulation bears striking resemblance to the P-F categories E-A, I-A, and M-A (Rosenzweig, 1967a). It is suggested that both the frustration theory which underlies the P-F Study and the broader triadic hypothesis may provide a well-formulated structure upon which to base further research in this area.

Indirect support for the triadic hypothesis has been afforded by investigations of extrasensory perception (ESP) which utilized the P-F Study (Schmeidler, 1950, 1954). Subjects who showed this special talent (guessed objects or numbers at a level greater than chance) were found to have significantly higher imaggression scores than subjects who demonstrated no special ability; subjects without ESP ability had significantly greater extraggression scores than subjects with ESP (Schmeidler, 1950). In another investigation a significant negative correlation was found between E-A and ESP scores (Eilbert and Schmeidler, 1950). A follow-up investigation discovered, however, that only those subjects who were mildly frustrated by their ESP tasks showed significant positive relationship between ESP and M-A scores and negative relationship between ESP and E-A scores (Schmeidler, 1954). It was suggested from the findings that, on the average, subjects with friendlier attitudes toward ESP (less E-A) are likely to show higher ESP scores than subjects who are hostile (more E-A) toward ESP (Schmeidler and McConnell, 1958). If ESP is conceptualized as an openness to external stimuli (similar to suggestibility), then a relationship can be seen with P-F construct-validity research involving the triadic hypothesis.

Factor Analysis

Attempts have been made from time to time to refine the structure of the P-F by the statistical procedure of factor analysis (Hayashi, Sumita, and Ichitani, 1959; Hayashi and Ichitani, 1970; Meyer and Schöfer, 1974), or to relate the P-F factors to other aspects of personality (Ichitani, 1966; Ichitani and Hayashi, 1976; Rauchfleisch, 1971b; Klippstein, 1972). The basic difference between instruments purporting to possess construct validity and those devised through statistical factor analysis is that the former proceed on a deductive basis and the latter on an inductive one. The hypothetical constructs of any projective technique need to be verified by examining the internal consistency of these constructs in structural terms and by experimental manipulations which put the constructs to the test of demonstrating their intrinsic merit. If such procedures are employed, the inductive approach to factor analysis is superfluous. Moreover, all the investigations cited above have been logically at fault in using data consisting of P-F scores for the derivation of statistical factors. One could conceivably go back to the 24 P-F items and score them in some manner independent of the P-F categories, in which case factor analysis would be logically possible. But the use of the P-F scores as such precludes factor analysis.

However, the kind of "configuration-frequency analysis" used by Rauchfleisch (1974) represents a constructive, psychodiagnostic approach which should not be confused with the typical factor-analytic investigations critically cited above. It should also be noted that some method of factor analysis or partial correlation might profitably be employed in future research to separate the relatively permanent vis-à-vis the situational components of the regular P-F scores.

Levels of Behavior

The concept of projection is inherent in the P-F since it was conceived as a semiprojective technique. The level of behavior indicates the manner in which projection is employed by the subject. Rosenzweig (1950b) postulated three such levels: *opinion*—reflecting self-critical, censored responses in keeping with one's self-image and norms of social propriety; *overt*—reflecting uncritical, everyday, observable reactions; and *implicit*—reflecting impersonal responses arising from latent or unconscious attitudes or feelings.

Rosenzweig (1945) originally presented the working hypothesis that the P-F reflects the actual (overt) behavior of the individual rather than his unconscious orientation. However, in later writings (for example, Rosenzweig, 1950b), he cautioned against the uncritical acceptance of this premise. He also warned against sole reliance upon the P-F in clinical psychodiagnosis and suggested that only if it were included in a battery of instruments and interpreted in connection with interview and case-history data would the P-F "find its own level." This view sparked a multifaceted approach to the problem of levels in the P-F.

Opinion Level

Rosenzweig (1960) matched an early experimental 32-item version of the P-F Study in its ordinary pictorial form (for children) with an open-ended questionnaire in an attempt to determine the relative efficacy of the two devices in predicting the everyday behavior of schoolchildren. The subjects, 40 children aged nine through 13, were first administered the P-F. Approximately four months later they were given the questionnaire. Teachers were then asked to indicate which one of the two responses for each item seemed to them more characteristic of the child's observed everyday behavior. The judges were unaware of the aim of the project or the source of the paired responses. The judgments of three teachers were combined and analyzed by the chi square technique. It was assumed that if there were no real differences between the P-F and the questionnaire, the judgments would distribute themselves equally. Analysis revealed that for 14 of the 32 items the P-F responses were significantly favored over the questionnaire ($p < .05$); on only one item was the questionnaire favored. When judgments for the 32 items as a whole were similarly treated, there resulted a predominance in favor of the P-F that was highly significant ($p < .01$). Substituting written for pictorial stimuli obviously damages the projective integrity of the P-F.

The effect induced on the projective nature of the P-F by modifying instructions to require forced choice of limited alternatives has also been explored. Wallon and Webb (1957) reported that scores for direction of aggression on a multiple-choice version of the P-F resembled "faking" behavior (opinion level) as compared to results on the P-F under standard conditions for a matched group. The important indication is that the objectified format stereotyped the reactions and tended to debase the results of the P-F, which under ordinary administration more fully reflects the overt level. Schwartz, Cohen, and Pavlik (1964) also employed a multiple-choice adaptation of the P-F which was group administered with uniform and controlled time per item. They found that modification of set produced differences in direction of aggression between subjects who scored high and those who scored low on the Minnesota Multiphasic Personality Inventory (MMPI) K-scale. Rosenzweig (1965), in a critical reply, demonstrated that the results were spurious because the method of group administration with uniform time limits constricted P-F responses in a non-idiodynamic manner, and the forced multiple-choice format led to such artifacts as abnormally high frequencies of imaggression and low frequencies of intraggression. When this research is thus reappraised, confirmation of Wallon and Webb's conclusions is obtained.

In an extensive investigation of various multiple-choice formats of the P-F matched against standard administration, Rosenzweig (1970b) showed that the essential advantages of the standard P-F are lost by any forced-choice procedure. This result occurred even when subjects were permitted to work at their own speed, each with a separate examination blank which was passed in as soon as completed. Significantly fewer extraggressive responses and more group-conformity responses were obtained under multiple-choice conditions as compared to standard ones. The conclusion was reached that despite the slightly more inconvenient form of the standard P-F (which, however, averages only 15 minutes in administration and can be scored with proficiency in about the same amount of time), its advantages for psychodiagnostic research far outweigh its disadvantages as compared to any more mechanized, multiple-choice version.

Overt Level vis-à-vis Other Levels

Rogers and Paul (1959) assumed that the P-F tapped the overt level, and attempted to predict, on the basis of psychoanalytic theory, the concomitant behavior expected at the implicit level. They advanced the hypothesis that "an extreme degree of conscious impunitiveness has a cognate substratum of unconscious aggressiveness" (p. 461). Subjects with high M-A scores on the P-F were found unwittingly to rate themselves as significantly more aggressive ($p < .05$) than did a control group during a tachistoscopic presentation. The interpretive meaning of the behavior tapped by the P-F accorded with the construct of repression: subjects with high M-A scores may be viewed as unconsciously repressing aggressiveness in order to maintain self-esteem. It is regrettable that the sample used in this investigation was small, but the methodology provides a model for potentially important further research.

A like investigation by Searle (1976) with 137 16-17-year-old subjects yielded reciprocal results. Extrapunitive scores on the P-F were coupled with self-ratings of aggressiveness, and the combination was related to ratings of characters in two commercial films (*Goldfinger,* a James Bond movie, and *The Comedians,* based on the spy novel by Graham Greene). It was found that subjects with high E scores on the P-F who rated themselves as low in hostility perceived the aggressive film characters as being more violent than did high-E subjects who rated themselves as high on hostility. The author concludes that this finding can be most readily explained by the classical psychoanalytic theory of projection: repression of hostility with lack of insight into the process leads to an exaggerated perception of hostility in others. The implication is that with certain individuals the P-F functions at the implicit level, which is then projected to the outside.

While the earlier study (Rogers and Paul, 1959) isolated subjects with high impunitive scores who were demonstrated to have unconsciously repressed extrapunitiveness, the later one (Searle, 1976) reciprocally isolated subjects with high extrapunitive scores but without insight into their hostility who then unconsciously projected this hostility onto other figures. It is evident from these two investigations that the P-F does in some instances tap the implicit level. To determine whether and in what way P-F scores reflect the implicit level may, however, require supplementary data. In careful clinical procedure, the inquiry at the end of the administration may contribute to this end.

Nencini and Misiti (1956b) administered the P-F to 20 subjects and asked them to respond with what they would have "said" in corresponding life situations; then the subjects were requested to say what they would have "thought" but not actually have said; finally they were asked to express their "opinion" of what would have been proper in each situation. When these results were compared with those of a control group which had been given a standard administration of the P-F, strong agreement was found between the "said" responses of the experimental group and responses of the control group. Experimental-group "thought" and "opinion" responses differed significantly ($p < .05$) from control-group responses. Bell and Rosenzweig (1965) reported that when P-F instructions were worded to decrease projective distance (to allow the subject greater identification with the situation), subjects gave more responses which they considered indicative of their everyday behavior than when instructions were worded to increase projective distance. Trentini (1961) found that the P-F scores of subjects who had been told that the results would affect their scholastic success did not significantly differ from scores of subjects who had been given the P-F anonymously. This finding is questionable since it has been demonstrated that, depending upon instructions, P-F scores are susceptible to faking (Silverstein, 1957; Wallon and Webb, 1957). Furthermore, as Mirmow (1952b) and Sutcliffe (1955) have shown, anonymous administration of the P-F encourages less socially conforming responses.

Verbal aggression as measuréd by the P-F may be regarded as a partial index of the individual's total aggression repertoire. This assumption has led investigators to employ a wide variety of criterion measures in attempts to match P-F scores with overt behavior. Mirmow (1952b) cites an unpublished investigation in which six clinical psychologists, who had worked together in the same laboratory for periods ranging from six months to three years, attempted to identify anonymous P-F protocols of their colleagues, administered before any of the participants were familiar with the instrument. Identification was accurate beyond the .01 level of chance expectancy. In a second investigation (Mirmow, 1952b) the P-F protocols of 25 hospitalized neurotic and psychotic patients were matched with qualitative summaries of their characteristic patterns of response in frustrating situations that had been written by the attending psychiatrists. The results showed overall matching to be successful ($p < .01$), but no compelling data concerning the validity of single aspects of the P-F were provided.

Albee and Goldman (1950) compared the P-F scores of 65 psychotic patients who had been classified as extraggressive or intraggressive on the basis of accident reports compiled by ward nurses. No reliable association was found between these classifications and P-F scores. This finding is not surprising in view of the complex relevance of the criterion (accidents) to patterns of reaction to interpersonal frustration presumably measured by the P-F. Other investigations, not reported here, have similar questionable features regarding the appropriateness of validating criteria (for example, Holzberg and Posner, 1951) or the reliability of criterion measures (for example, Pareek, 1964).

Lindzey and Goldwyn (1954) compared the E-A scores of 20 college students with independent measures of the three above-described behavioral levels. The only significant correlation ($p < .05$) was between observer ratings and E-A scores. Christiansen (1959) administered a Norwegian adaptation of the P-F to 136 subjects, then a five-point rating scale to determine the level of responses. He reported that the overt level was used by subjects most frequently though few subjects maintained this level consistently throughout the Study. The P-F was also found to correlate highly with a previously administered inventory of everyday reactions. Nisenson (1972) examined aggressive reactions to frustration in relation to levels of extrapunitiveness of subjects in catharsis and noncatharsis conditions. He found that "the P-F Study did a creditable job in selecting individuals who display predictable and graded amounts of aggression in response to frustrations" (p. 53).

Implicit Level

Rosenzweig (1960) reported an investigation by Wechsberg in which the children's form of the P-F was used to determine the level of behavior (opinion or implicit) evoked in normal as compared to maladjusted subjects. (No measure of the overt level was included.) Intraindividual analysis of the results showed that normal subjects had clearly differentiated implicit and opinion levels, and some agreement between P-F results and scores on a self-concept questionnaire was found. The maladjusted children exhibited no consistent differences between behavior levels and had P-F scores which more closely resembled measures of fantasy behavior. Lockwood (1975) found that allowing children openly to express their fantasies after a frustrating situation produced a set in which similar fantasy material was expressed on the P-F.

Given the shared dynamics underlying the P-F and other projective techniques which more directly purport to discern personality structure, it has been naively assumed that these latter instruments should correlate with the P-F. Lindzey and Tejessy (1956) were concerned with the problem of behavior levels in regard to both the TAT and the P-F. They found that "signs" of aggression on the TAT correlated significantly ($p < .05$) with self-ratings and with E-A and I-A scores on the P-F although little relation was found between these signs and observer ratings, or ratings assigned by a diagnostic council. However, the specific criteria from which the various ratings were derived were questionable and any conclusions drawn from this investigation are, at best, tenuous.

Schwartz (1952) discovered few significant relationships between P-F and Rorschach scores although E-A, I-A, and N-P correlated significantly with items on the the Sheviakov and Friedberg Interest Inventory. Palmer (1957), however, compared experience-balance scores on the Rorschach with P-F category scores and tentatively concluded that Rorschach perceptual modes are parallel to P-F reaction types. Lindzey and Goldwyn (1954) obtained no significant correlation between E-A scores on the P-F and a word-association technique which was assumed to tap implicit behavior. In an investigation involving 121 state prison inmates, Kaswan, Wasman, and Freedman (1960) related E-A scores on the P-F to 22 measures of aggression derived from the Rorschach, an attitude scale, a psychiatric-interview schedule, and case-history data. Chi square comparison between high E-A scores and the aggression measures showed ten statistically significant relationships. The authors concluded that the P-F has a meaningful relation to other measures of aggression although a meaningful pattern of test-criterion relations was still to be determined.

The preceding investigations offer a basic framework within which the problem of levels of behavior can be explored with any technique. As regards the P-F it is clear that no unequivocal general conclusion can be reached at this point. We can say that the standard P-F, by virtue of its construction, yields results which diverge from opinion behavior. The pictorial format—which allows the subject to identify with the frustrated individual—and nonrestrictive demands concerning response—which allow the subject to answer in terms of his idiodynamic orientation—combine to make the P-F something other than an assessor of self-critical response. Multiple-choice variants of the P-F constrain the subject's expression of reaction to frustration since these choices cannot encompass the multiplicity of psychologically real combinations of types and directions of aggression. Changes in percentage for direction of aggression (lowered E-A and increased I-A or M-A, depending upon instructions) and group conformity (increased GCR) are found with such modified versions. The use of a questionnaire or forced-choice format must therefore be rejected since such modifications encourage "faked" behavior, contradict the intended projective nature of the instrument, and reduce diagnostic usefulness by promoting an exclusively demographic orientation (Rosenzweig, 1965).

The research, confirming Rosenzweig's early hypothesis, demonstrates that the P-F operates by and large (not exclusively) at the overt level in normal populations. Nevertheless, it has proved difficult to confirm this proposition by comparing P-F scores with independent measures of overt behavior. Some investigators have shown little understanding of P-F constructs by selecting behavioral criteria which are only remotely related to interpersonal frustration or which, due to their situation specificity, provide a poor index of the individual's aggression repertoire. Types of aggression on the P-F are also often excluded from comparison. Finally, the reliability of the criterion measures employed is often inadequate or suspect.

The findings regarding the relationship of the P-F with other projective and semiprojective methods (assumed to tap the implicit level) are generally inconclusive. In view of the ineffective or nonexistent control for level of behavior in research comparing these techniques, the fact that any significant correlations are found among methods reveals little and is somewhat gratuitous. Furthermore, since such tools as the TAT and the Rorschach do not provide direct measures of aggression, the skill of the clinician in interpreting results plays a large and undefined part in determining whether relationships with other instruments will be discovered. Order of technique presentation can also have a bearing on results. For example, preceding the P-F with the TAT was found significantly to increase P-F scores for extraggression (Berkun and Burdick, 1964). A final problem is that attempts to validate an instrument by comparing it with other methods which themselves have questionable or limited validity produce results which are uncertain and open to misinterpretation. Correlations among projective techniques are therefore useful only when interpreted in the context of more systematic construct-validity research.

Overt behavior is not necessarily reflected in the P-F protocols of normal subjects. The results of previous research on felons and delinquents (Rosenzweig, 1963) suggest that such subjects may often produce either implicit or opinion behavior. Obviously, motivational factors, especially social desirability, affect level of behavior and must always be considered in clinical interpretation.

Though not directly concerned with the issue of levels, the modification of the original P-F Study instructions to omit the phrase "avoid being humorous" should be mentioned here. In an investigation specifically directed to this problem (Rosenzweig, 1950f) it was demonstrated that it is immaterial whether subjects respond humorously or not, since humorous responses lend themselves as readily as do nonhumorous ones to scoring in P-F terms. Consequently the admonition not to be humorous was omitted from the adult form instructions beginning in 1950, and a corresponding change was made in the children's form. But the point worth emphasizing here is that this work disclosed by serendipity a classification of humor corresponding to the three chief types encountered on the stage or, for that matter, in everyday life: extrapunitive humor, directed against someone or something external to the speaker and made by him into the butt of the joke; intropunitive humor, directed against the speaker himself in a pseudomasochistic fashion; impunitive humor, the nonsense variety in which embarrassment is glossed over by dissipating anxiety into harmless channels. Though it has long been known that humor is closely tied to frustration, the classification afforded by the categories of the P-F had not hitherto been spelled out. This discovery adds an incidental dimension to the presumed construct validity of the instrument.

To confirm this aspect of validity requires further systematic research, both with the P-F and with any necessary related experimental or diagnostic procedures. The three types of humor might thus be explored and more critically defined, not only for the understanding of the aggression categories but as a contribution to the knowledge of humor itself as a form of behavior related to the experience of frustration.

Experimental Induction of Frustration

The constructs of the P-F emerged in part from experimental research on frustration associated with task completion and incompletion under conditions of varying ego-involvement. Further validation of these constructs is possible by making the P-F a dependent variable for determining changes in reaction to frustration after a period of intervening stress.

Lange (cited in Mirmow, 1952b) administered the P-F to two comparable groups of college students on two occasions separated by a six-week interval. For the experimental group the second administration took place immediately following a 24-hour period of sleep deprivation. Results for the control group showed little change from first to second examination, but for the experimental group, scores showed a significant increase in ego (etho)-defense, a decrease in obstacle-dominance and intraggression, and a tendency toward higher extraggression. The shift from O-D to E-D indicated greater defensiveness after frustration while the decrease in I-A and rise in E-A were suggestive of regression to a more primitive response pattern. Loveland and Singer (1959) found no significant differences on either the P-F or the Rorschach between a group of soldiers deprived of sleep for 98 hours and a control group. However, the questionable procedure of administering the same tests three times to each group within a span of only one week tends to depreciate the findings. Franklin and Brozek (1949) reported that the P-F showed no effect of the frustration associated with conditions of semistarvation. Methodological considerations involving the motivation of the experimental group and a lack of experimental control again raise questions regarding the findings.

Lindzey (1950b) reported an increase in E-A following exposure to a series of biologically and socially frustrating situations. French (1950) tested 80 students three weeks before and immediately following the return of a course examination on which grades had been deliberately falsified. While differences between good and poor students were absent at the time of the initial P-F administration, the poor students—presumably more vulnerable to the stress attendant upon the reception of the poor grades—showed greater extraggression and less intropersistence on the second P-F. Pareek (1964) administered the Indian adaptation of the children's form to 50 boys 12 years of age, first under normal conditions and then, two weeks later, after a frustrating intelligence test. He found a significant increase in E-A ($p < .05$) and O-D ($p < .01$) and a decrease in I-A ($p < .01$) and E-D ($p < .01$) on the second administration. Unfortunately no control was included in this investigation.

In general, the research indicates that imposed external stress tends to result in a mean increase in extraggression and a decrease in intraggression. Conclusions regarding type of aggression are not as clear. The main effects of frustration seem centered on the more primitive O-D and E-D types of reaction rather than the more developed, constructive N-P. Contradictory findings are probably due to differences in the maturity of individual subjects, the idiodynamic meaning of the frustrating intervention, and the subject's initial set.

Findings in general indicate that reactions to frustration arise from a combination of situational and dynamic components. Although all P-F categories have been shown to have significant retest reliability (Rosenzweig, Ludwig, and Adelman, 1975), the average retest reliability of categories ranges from .50 to .66, with direction of aggression having higher values and types of aggression, lower values. If aggression were an invariant personality trait, one would expect retest correlations approaching 1.00. Retest correlations of the magnitude reported, however, are in keeping with assumptions concerning the interaction effect, since significant stability is shown in regard to typical mode of reaction while a large part of the remaining variance represents situational factors. On the whole, the above-reported investigations tend to confirm this view and to that extent lend support to the construct validity of the P-F.

Physiological Correlates of P-F Aggression Categories

The dynamic theory from which the P-F took its impetus was formulated from a psychobiological perspective. Rosenzweig (1944) stressed the importance of levels of defense as an intrinsic aspect of frustration theory. It is therefore not surprising that physiological correlates have been found for P-F constructs.

Funkenstein, King, and Drolette (1957) reported that students who, when placed in stressful (frustrating) situations, responded with Anger-Out (E-A) or with No-Emotion (M-A), had low-intensity physiological reactions, and gave evidence of excessive secretions of a norepinephrinelike substance. Those who reacted with Anger-In (I-A) showed high-intensity physiological reactions and secretion of an epinephrinelike substance. The authors suggested that extraggression is a more primitive form of response in which anger is expressed outward, away from the self, with little need for emergency reaction. Intraggression, on the other hand, represents a more "civilized" response in which retroflexed anger presents a real threat to the self and thus necessitates an emergency response. *Schildkraut and Kety (1967)* discussed much of the research which supports the hypothesis that norepinephrine is related to outwardly aggressive behavior (E-A in the P-F) while epinephrine is related to passively anxious behavior (I-A).

Attempts to match aggressive personality traits to catecholamine excretion *(Silverman, Cohen, Zuidema, and Lazar, 1957; Frankenhaeuser and Kareby, 1962)* have produced equivocal results, in part because of the different methods of personality assessment employed and, possibly, because of a neglect of cross-cultural differences. Fine and Sweeney (1968) found that the norepinephrine-epinephrine ratio (NE/E), rather than norepinephrine or epinephrine separately, was more apposite in distinguishing between individuals rated high and low on trait aggressiveness as derived from a modified TAT. Results concerning the P-F were inconclusive (although in the expected direction: NE/E appeared directly related to E-A and inversely related to I-A). The authors incorrectly assumed that the P-F consistently measures personality traits or types and, therefore, adopted a methodology in which catecholamine samples were not collected during the same time frame in which the P-F was administered. In contrast to such measures as the Allport A-S Reaction Study *(Allport, 1928)* which, by definition, assess relatively permanent personality traits, the P-F Study investigates types of reaction to frustration that may have some personal consistency over time but are not conceived to be uninfluenced by situational determinants. In P-F terms one might well expect Fine and Sweeney to conclude that NE/E is meaningfully related to the interaction of specific stress situations (as idiodynamically experienced) and the relatively stable aggressive dynamics of the person.

CONCLUSION

A schema for assessing the validity of semiprojective techniques has been advanced in which two provinces were delineated: primary, consisting of construct and criterion-related validity, in which the major focus is either on the soundness and self-consistency of the technique in relation to its underlying concepts or on the relationship between tool results and specified external variables; and secondary, consisting of pragmatic validity, that is, tool appropriateness and the usefulness of the instrument in applied areas. Feedback from secondary investigation can lead to further primary research and may also define the limits of tool applicability. In all such validity research it should be recognized that projective and semiprojective techniques are tools, not mainly psychometric tests in the usual sense. The skill of the examiner or clinician is an integral part of the instrument-in-operation, and this fact should be more explicitly acknowledged and included in validation research.

The construct-validity model was applied in assessing the validity of the Rosenzweig P-F Study with the following results:

1. Expected developmental patterns are reflected in normative data.
2. P-F constructs form organized score patterns which are related to basic frustration theory.
3. Factor analysis is largely irrelevant to the validation of hypothetico-deductive instruments like the P-F.
4. The P-F is to be construed as operative at the overt level of behavior but with other levels always available for particular subjects or items.
5. Verbal aggression only partially generalizes to other overt behavior.
6. Exposure to intervening stress leads to measurable changes in P-F scores.
7. P-F constructs represent an interaction of situational behaviors with personality characteristics stable over time.
8. Physiological correlates exist for P-F directions of aggression.

More support has been generated for the validity of directions than for types of aggression. A basic problem has been the lack of recognition of the affirmative (constructive) aspects of aggression along with undue emphasis on destructive effects. Future research which explores the balance between etho (ego)-defense and behavioral persistence toward solutions despite frustration is highly desirable.

4   Criterion-Related and Pragmatic Validity

It will be recalled that criterion-related validity is established by relating an instrument to criteria derived either from other psychodiagnostic tests, from behavioral ratings, or from culturally defined status differences. Thus, for the P-F Study comparison has been made with behavioral ratings or, again, with data from personality inventories. In a somewhat different approach work has centered on groups differentiated according to culturally defined levels of aggressiveness. The major findings under these two approaches are presented here.

COMPARISON WITH CRITERIA FROM OTHER TESTS

The relationships of P-F scores to aggression ratings derived from overt behavior or from projective methods other than the P-F have been found to involve a determination of the level at which the P-F operates vis-à-vis these criteria. For this reason the findings in these two areas have already been reviewed under construct validity. It remains to consider here the result achieved from comparisons with psychometric test data.

Various investigators have compared P-F Study results with scores derived from personality and adjustment inventories. One early attempt (Falls and Blake, 1949) involved correlating directions of aggression and the GCR on the P-F with scores on the MMPI, the Bernreuter Personality Inventory (BPI), the Bell Adjustment Inventory, the Allport-Vernon Study of Values, and several measures of intelligence and socioeconomic status. Positive relationships were found between E-A percent on the P-F and both general and social maladjustment as measured by the Bell Adjustment Inventory. Imaggression, while negatively related to depression and hysteria on the MMPI and to social maladjustment on the Bell, was positively related to dominance on the BPI. The GCR was positively associated with scholastic achievement and with the dominance scale of the BPI and negatively associated with hypochondriasis on the MMPI and religious values on the Allport-Vernon. The authors concluded that the projective methods of assessing personality, as exemplified by the P-F, tend to be "functionally related" to the more strictly psychometric measures. Shupp (as reported by Mirmow, 1952b) and Quay and Sweetland (1954) were unable to duplicate these findings with the BPI and MMPI, respectively. Conceptual flaws, however, tend to invalidate these later negative results. For example, Quay and Sweetland proceeded from the simplistic hypothesis that E-A and I-A are signs of emotional maladjustment, and M-A, of adjustment.

But the majority of investigations do show relationships between the P-F Study and psychometric personality tests. Karlin and Schwartz (1953) reported significant results which suggested that ability indices derived from the George Washington University Social Intelligence Test and the Otis Mental Abilities Test are related to type of reaction to frustration. Cognizance of a speaker's mental state was found to be positively related to I-A and M-A scores and negatively related to E-A scores while general intelligence was related to sizing up the problem aspect of a situation (O-D) and going on to find solutions (N-P). The P-F has also shown itself to be sensitive to personal feelings of security and insecurity. Students who scored high and low in security on Maslow's SI (Security-Insecurity) Inventory displayed significant differences in E-A and M-A scores; the insecure group was more extraggressive and less imaggressive (Bennett and Jordan, 1958). During the same time period, an investigation with 157 fifth-grade children showed that the P-F Study was able to reflect differences in two groups who had scored high and low on a questionnaire of punishment merited for misbehavior (Levitt and Lyle, 1955). Children scoring high in punitiveness displayed significantly more extraggression and obstacle-dominance and less intraggression than did the P-F normative group; children low in punitiveness showed less ego- or etho-defense and more need-persistence than the normative sample. Groups of poorly adjusted, averagely adjusted, and well adjusted pupils have also been significantly differentiated by their P-F scores for categories I-A, M-A, and GCR (Smith, 1958). Recent work with adults has demonstrated significant relationships between directions of aggression and personality factors. Schalock and MacDonald (1966) administered the P-F Study and the (Cattell) Sixteen Personality Factor Questionnaire to 164 high school and college students. It was found that extraggression is related to suspiciousness, anxiety, and tenseness in males; intraggression is related negatively to suspiciousness for both sexes; and imaggression, negatively related to adventurousness in females and positively related to self-confidence in males. Similarly, Mooney Problem Check List variables—courtship, sex, and marriage; morals and religion; home and family—were shown to have a negative relation to P-F extraggression scores in a group of juvenile offenders (Mukerji and Debabrata, 1968).

SUCCESSIVE CLINICAL PREDICTIONS

The method of successive clinical predictions (Rosenzweig, 1950c) has been employed to assess the criterion-related validity of the P-F Study with both psychometric and projective test data (Mirmow—see Rosenzweig, 1960). A number of investigators, in conference, attempt to predict, on the basis of anamnestic and psychological test results with which they are provided, the P-F scores of unknown subjects. In Mirmow's investigation the attempt was made to predict the scores of 24 children. Prediction followed from previously formulated hypotheses but such hypotheses could be accepted, rejected, or revised during the conferences. Given a succession of predictions it was assumed that the P-F, if valid at all, would gradually define its own validity, and that the judges would become more accurate in their predictions. Blind identification of the total P-F protocol was found to be significantly more successful for the last nine than for the first ten subjects on whom this task was performed. Furthermore, in ten of 19 cases the composite judgment correctly identified the P-F of the subject (Chi square significant, $p < .01$). Correlations of composite predictions and actual scores revealed significant correspondence for P-F categories E-A, I-A, M-A, and GCR, but the coefficients for types of aggression were not significant.

These findings indicate that certain P-F category scores are related to personality and ability measures derived from psychometric tests. Prediction of other behavior from isolated category scores is, however, hazardous since only a limited picture of the individual's total reaction to frustration is thus made available. While it may be possible to utilize single scores or aspects of the P-F for comparative purposes, exclusive reliance on such a procedure tends to debase the semiprojective nature of the technique by stressing group norms and disregarding the information to be gained through examination of the configuration of responses. The method of successive clinical predictions has provided a more sophisticated demonstration of the global predictive validity of the P-F Study.

GROUP DIFFERENCES

Criminals or Delinquents vis-à-vis Normals

The criminal or delinquent is generally considered in Western culture (in social, if not in legal, terms) as one who displays a higher level of hostility than that found in the population generally. Based on this cultural definition, research has been undertaken to determine whether the P-F Study significantly reflects the assumed aggressiveness differences between normals and offenders.

Findings from investigations comparing the P-F scores of adult prison inmates with those of matched control groups or normative data have been inconclusive. In an early investigation, college students were found to exhibit significantly higher extraggression and lower intraggression than prisoners (Fry, 1949). However, the lack of comparability of the two groups with respect to age, social status, and educational level makes interpretation of these findings difficult. No significant P-F differences were found in a comparison of psychopaths and physically assaultive prisoners with matched groups of normals (Holzberg and Hahn, 1952; Mercer and Kyriazis, 1962). On the other hand, an investigation of two groups of Polish offenders, one with concentration-camp experience and the other with a background of forced labor in industry or agriculture, revealed no significant P-F differences but did demonstrate elevated extraggression scores for both groups (Grygier, 1954). Further examination of the P-F scores of delinquent and nondelinquent displaced persons showed that delinquents tended to be more extraggressive and less intraggressive and imaggressive. This investigation is, however, weakened by small and unequal numbers of subjects in sample groups and by poor matching of subjects.

Findings similar to the above can be extracted from the research of Kaswan, Wasman, and Freedman (1960). They reported that high extraggression scores of 121 prison inmates were related to various other aggression measures. In contradiction to this result, Megargee (1966b) cited an investigation in which extremely assaultive prisoners had significantly lower E-A scores than other prisoners or normals. He was unable to substantiate this result in his own research and, instead, found that prisoners gave "faked" answers—displaying decreased E-A and increased GCR—on the P-F. (The ability of subjects to manipulate some of their P-F behavior so as to make a good or bad impression has been recognized [Rosenzweig, 1950b; Silverstein, 1957].)

Results from investigations which employed the adult form of the P-F with juvenile delinquents have been equally mixed. Delinquent girls were reported to exhibit lower E-A and GCR scores and higher I-A and M-A scores than nondelinquents (Vane, 1954; Sivanandam, 1971). An obvious explanation for these results is the tendency of delinquents to try to appear respectable. On the other hand, Towner (as reported by Mirmow, 1952b) found that delinquent boys had significantly lower I scores than normals. This result was seen as supporting the view that delinquents are lacking in feelings of guilt and self-blame. To confuse the situation further, Norman and Kleinfeld (1958) found no significant differences between the P-F scores of 20 delinquents and 22 control-group subjects, all Spanish-American males. In an effort to explain this failure, Swickard and Spilka (1961) administered the P-F Study, the Siegel Manifest Hostility Scale, and a 39-item Social Desirability Scale extracted from the MMPI to 74 male and female delinquents, 37 Spanish-American and 37 non-Spanish white. Taking into account the tendency of delinquents to make a good impression on personality measures, the authors corrected both the Siegel Scale and the P-F for social desirability. No significant differences between groups emerged for adjusted P-F means on direction of aggression although the groups were significantly differentiated on the adjusted Manifest Hostility scores.

The children's form of the P-F has also been used in the investigation of behavior problems and delinquency. Research on 32 boys with adjustment problems (Ferguson, 1954) disclosed elevated extraggression and low GCR scores. Investigations which employed matched control groups instead of standardization-norm data for comparative purposes have, however, shown the delinquents to have less extraggression than normals, though with no differences in GCR (Lindzey and Goldwyn, 1954; Singh, Paliwal, and Gupta, 1972). But Pareek (1964) reported no significant differences for either direction or type of aggression in a comparison of the P-F scores of 20 delinquents with the normal-group data collected for the Indian adaptation of the children's form of the P-F. These delinquents had significantly lower GCR scores than the normal group.

The preceding investigations have focused on individual P-F category scores in making comparisons between groups. A promising new method of exploring group differences by utilizing clusters of P-F factor and category scores has been demonstrated by Rauchfleisch (1973, 1974, 1976). He analyzed P-F results and IQ scores in terms of "configuration frequency" and applied this technique in an investigation of 189 delinquents. Three typical and recurrent delinquent personality profiles were disclosed: low IQ, low E', high I and M; low IQ, low E, M, and i, high E' and I'; high IQ, low I', M, and N-P, high E. Rauchfleisch's approach is important because it points up the conceptual naïveté of others who tend to treat delinquency as a monolithic entity.

Part of the problem involved in many of the preceding investigations of juvenile delinquency has been the utilization of an approximate instrument. Since the adolescent form of the P-F is of only recent availability (Rosenzweig, 1970a), most previous research has employed either the adult or children's form in work with teenagers. The children's form (Rosenzweig, 1977a), however, is strictly applicable only through age 13 and the adult form (Rosenzweig, 1978b), though initially standardized for the age span 14 through 19, is now superseded for this teenage period by the adolescent form (Rosenzweig, 1976c). Even more basic questions have been raised concerning much of the work done with felons and delinquents (Rosenzweig, 1963). Most investigators take little account of the three levels of behavior—opinion, overt, implicit—which a semiprojective device, such as the P-F, may tap (Rosenzweig, 1950b). Assaultive delinquents, accustomed to publicly denying their hostile attitudes, would, at the opinion level, obtain normal or even better-than-normal extraggression scores. The P-F scores of delinquents may also reflect attempts to make oneself look good in anticipation of rewards for doing so. The further possibility exists that, at the implicit level, some criminals may actually be more intraggressive than normals (as in the psychoanalytic concept of "criminality from a sense of guilt") so that, if responding at this level, these subjects would receive higher intraggression scores than normals. It may well be the exception rather than the rule (as advanced in the discussion of construct validity) to find delinquents performing on the P-F at the overt level assumed in their culturally defined status. A further consideration is the problematic use of the word "delinquent" to cover a very wide variety of antisocial behaviors. Rauchfleisch has aptly shown that there are many types of delinquents with varying aggression profiles. One must also determine the degree to which aggression expressed by delinquents and felons is socially conditioned by specific frustrating situations which the P-F does not necessarily or fully comprehend.

When viewed with these qualifications the preceding investigations appear to demonstrate that the P-F, though sensitive to aggression differences, has not been optimally used. If motivational variables affecting level of behavior are considered and groups are more adequately matched, one may anticipate more consistent and theoretically intelligible P-F results. A definitive conclusion on this aspect of P-F criterion-related validity must await further and sounder research.

Athletes vis-à-vis Nonathletes

Athletic activity is often narrowly conceptualized as a socially accepted channeling of hostile impulses. However, a broader conceptualization of aggression, like that incorporated in the P-F Study, requires the acknowledgment of positive, constructive acts which give expression to aggressive energy. In these terms the self-discipline of the athlete—his ability to train toward a goal—needs to be considered along with his competitive or directly hostile behavior.

Various investigators have used the P-F to compare athletes with nonathletes. A major focus has been boxing since the hostile aggression of the boxer is at the root of his sport; hostility is not secondary to some other goal as is the case, for example, in football. A study of highly successful 1960 Italian Olympic boxers revealed that fighters were significantly more extrapunitive and ego-defensive than groups in a normative sample (Riccio and Antonelli, 1962). These boxers showed less obstacle-dominance and need-persistence. Mastruzzo (1964) similarly found that boxers exhibit more E-A and less I-A, M-A, and O-D than control groups. In his sample, however, boxers showed more need-persistence than control groups.

Confusion is introduced when the results of an investigation of American college boxers, cross-country runners, and control groups are considered (Husman, 1955). These boxers showed the least extraggression of all these groups and they tended to direct their hostility inward (I-A) or to turn it off (M-A). After a fight the boxers scored higher on super-ego factors, presumably an indication of a sense of guilt. Cross-country runners exhibited the greatest amount of E-A of all the groups. The inconsistent P-F results with Italian and with American boxers may reflect cross-cultural differences in the role of the boxer or changes in aggressive reactions with increasing level of skill; or they may be an artifact of repeated P-F testing done with the American group.

A study of an allied sport, fencing, revealed that Italian fencers exhibit P-F patterns similar to the findings with Italian boxers: increased extrapunitiveness and ego-defense, and decreased intraggression and need-persistence (Antonelli, Tuccimei, and Celli, 1964). Soccer, basketball, and volleyball players in the Soviet Union (Hanin, 1976) have been studied by means of the P-F but the results are not available for reporting at this time. Aggressive reactions of football players in the United States have been explored by Schneider (1974). From a carefully designed investigation of 48 team members who were repeatedly (perhaps too frequently) retested, to include the effects of game-winning and game-losing experiences, the author concludes that verbally aggressive (antisocial) behavior is intensified rather than diminished during the football season.

Athletes who compete in different sports which require great self-discipline and emotional control have been found to have similar P-F patterns. For example, both weightlifters and cyclists displayed less

E-A and E-D and more I-A and N-P than the normative sample (Rapi-sarda and Mastruzzo, 1960a, 1960b). Athletes in these sports appear to be successful only when they have developed self-control and the ability to withstand fatigue and physical pain.

Recent work by Figler (1976) has attempted to investigate the relationship between aggressive and athletic behavior by reexamining the conceptualization of aggression. The P-F Study was used as a primary means to this end. A distinction was made between Reactive (ego-involved) and Instrumental (problem-solving) aggressiveness, along the lines of the P-F distinction between etho-defensiveness and need-persistence. From a study involving 377 senior high school students it was concluded that maleness is associated with significantly greater Reactivity, but that athletic involvement does not distinguish among subjects in this regard. Male athletes were found to be significantly less Instrumentally aggressive than females and somewhat less than male nonathletes. Consideration was also given to the relationships between aggressiveness and type of sport preferred, with sports defined as to degree of physical interpersonal contact. The investigator concluded that while maleness is associated with greater Reactive aggressiveness, further investigation is needed to clarify the relationships between athletic involvement and both Reactive and Instrumental aggressiveness. Such work is in progress.

From this cursory survey of what are clearly exploratory researches, it may still be concluded that the P-F is a promising tool for the understanding of aggression in athletics and sports.

Males vis-à-vis Females

A basic societal assumption, recently subjected to vigorous questioning, is that males are more outwardly aggressive than females. This presupposition of aggression differences between the sexes would be expected to manifest itself on the P-F in higher E-A and E-D scores for males and in higher I-A, M-A, and GCR scores for females. In order to determine whether the P-F Study differentiates the sexes in these or other ways, data obtained both by standardization research and other investigations will be presented. In the present discussion of sex differences no assumptions are made as to their possible genesis. The focus is on empirical differences as they appear in relation to age and development.

Children's Form

In general, no significant sex differences have been found with the children's form of the P-F. Rosenzweig (1977a) reported no such differences in the norms for this form. Again, no significant sex differences were discovered when the protocols of elementary school children were scored and compared as to category (Spache, 1951; Stoltz and Smith, 1959). An investigation of 38 normal and 38 handicapped children similarly revealed no sex differences (Lynch and Arndt, 1973). In cross-cultural investigations significant sex differences could be found neither in a group of 714 German youths (Simons, 1967b) nor in a group of 80 Guatemalan boys and girls (Adinolfi, Watson, and Klein, 1973).

When the P-F has been analyzed in respect to specific frustrater-frustratee situations some sex differences have appeared (Spache, 1951). However, the nature of the specific status confrontation appears to affect both sexes equally. When frustrated by peers both sexes showed increased extraggression and etho-defense, whereas frustration by adults led to greater expression of intraggression, obstacle-dominance, and need-persistence. In verification of these findings, Stoltz and Smith (1959) discovered no significant sex differences in child-frustrater vis-à-vis adult-frustrater situations. But they did find that children polarize the presence of frustrating obstacles, and direct blame upon themselves when frustrated by adults and turn blame outward when frustrated by a (less threatening) peer.

Adolescent Form

Sex differences have been found in work with the adolescent form of the P-F. Rosenzweig and Braun (1970) reported an investigation involving 224 tenth- and twelfth-grade students in which males were found to be significantly more extraggressive and etho-defensive than females; females were significantly more intraggressive, imaggressive, need-persistent, and group conforming than males. (Similar results have been reported by Leonardi [1973] and Sharma [1975].) In accordance with Spache's (1951) findings, a further analysis was carried out to discover possible differences in relation to frustrater status. Both sexes showed a significant increase in E-A and E-D and a decrease in I-A and N-P when an adult was the frustrater as compared to when a peer was. The authors point out that further systematic research into the interaction of the sex of the subject and the age level of the pictured frustrater and frustratee is desirable.

Sex differences have also been revealed in the normative data collected for the adolescent form (Rosenzweig, 1970a). Males from ages 12 to 14 years, six months show significantly ($p < .05$) higher E-A percent and lower I-A percent than corresponding females. From ages 14 years, 7 months to 16 years, six months males exhibit significantly ($p < .01$) higher E-A percent and E-D percent and lower I-A percent, M-A percent, N-P percent, and GCR percent than females. These significant differences are maintained through age 18 years, 12 months.

The preceding results confirm the prevailing view that males become more outwardly aggressive than females during adolescence, possibly as a function of their greater competitiveness with the older generation. Not surprisingly, teenagers see adults as more threatening than peers.

Adult Form

In general, no consistent sex differences have been found in work with the adult form of the P-F. Normative data (Rosenzweig, 1978b) reveal no significant sex differences for any of the scoring categories. Results concerning sex differences among college students have been mixed. Bernard (1949) found males to be significantly more extraggressive than females, but Moore and Schwartz (1963) discovered no consistent sex differences in their sample of 201 college students. Since Bernard did not report the ages of his subjects, his results are ambiguous and may reflect late-adolescent differences. Examination of adult norms indicates that once the turbulence of teenage years has passed, both males and females exhibit similar patterns of reacting to frustration, at least through middle age. More data will be necessary before definitive statements can be made concerning older adults.

The P-F thus appears to be sensitive to sex differences in aggression. The research indicates that males and females differ significantly on the type of verbal aggression tapped by the P-F only during adolescence. During childhood and adulthood, normal individuals of both sexes undergo the same developmental pattern in regard to reaction to frustration. Further changes may, however, occur in late maturity. Since developmental aspects of aggression are involved in underlying P-F theory, this topic was previously discussed under construct validity.

PRAGMATIC VALIDITY

Pragmatic-validity research attempts to assess the utility of an instrument for selection or screening in various social settings. Since all practical applications begin with tacit acceptance of the construct and criterion-related validity of a technique, these investigations cannot be conceived as shedding any direct light on primary validity. Instead pragmatic investigations illuminate the ostensible purview of the technique; that is, they disclose those settings in which the device is presumably appropriate or useful, and thereby secondarily define more closely the areas of further fruitful primary-validity research. The most frequent social settings in which the P-F has been employed, and which will be reviewed here are business and industry, schools, courts and prisons, hospitals and clinics, and cultures (national and cross-cultural settings).

Business and Industry

The most frequent use of the P-F in business settings has been for personnel screening and selection. Scores on the P-F have been compared with ratings of job efficiency or other measures of performance, and then attempts were made to select likely candidates for promotion. Sinaiko (1949), in an early investigation, examined the ability of the P-F to predict job performance of department store section managers. When job-performance scores were correlated with P-F categories it was found that M-A correlated positively with length of service on the job; I-A and N-P correlated positively with job ratings; E-A correlated negatively with job ratings. These findings are consistent with expectations since the good salesman must suppress overt aggression ("the customer is always right") and persist toward his final goal. When P-F scores were combined into an index, a cutting score was achieved which admitted ten of the 15 top-rated section managers and eliminated 11 of the 15 bottom-rated ones. Similarly, in a selection process for probationary police officers, it was found that E-D and I-A scores could be used with other psychological test data to produce a multiple-correlation coefficient which significantly predicted the service record (DuBois and Watson, 1950). More recently the P-F has been used to predict job success among engineering inspectors (Perczel and Perczel, 1969) and salesmen (Van Dam, 1970). The latter investigation confirmed Sinaiko's findings: successful salesmen tend to be high in imaggression and need-persistence and low in extraggression and etho-defense.

Attempts have also been made to use the P-F as a military screening device. In Belgium the P-F was found of little use in selecting army officers (Delys and Zeghers, 1955), but in France the P-F was successfully used to distinguish between cadets who were dropped and those who were retained as pilots in an army air corps program (Boisbourdin, Michel, and Peltier, 1956). Cadets who had been retained in the program demonstrated a significantly higher GCR percentage and lower frequency of unscoreable responses than cadets who were eliminated. In the United States, Wallon (1956) found no significant P-F differences between naval aviation cadets who completed and those who withdrew from a flight training program. However, cadets who withdrew early in training were significantly more extraggressive than cadets who withdrew later. Intraggression was also positively correlated with length of time in the program among those who ultimately withdrew.

Schools

Achievement

Investigations which have employed the P-F to determine whether high achievers and underachievers in schools show different patterns of reaction to frustration have produced fairly consistent results. In an early study (Junken, 1953) the P-F scores of sixth-grade pupils who had been reported as academically advanced were compared with the scores of children reported to be academically retarded. No significant P-F differences were found between the two groups. It was believed, however, that the basis for achievement might lie in differential frustration reactions to persons with varying authority. A further P-F breakdown into specific frustrater situations (similar to that in Spache, 1951) was performed and the analysis then yielded significant findings. The advanced group, as compared to the low achievers, showed greater extraggression in response to peer-induced frustration and had more trends toward E-A in adult-frustrater situations. The low achievers, as compared to the high achievers, exhibited greater imaggression in adult-frustrater situations. It would appear that children who are more free to express aggression when frustrated by adults are more able to achieve academically than those who resort to evasion in such situations.

Support for this view was generated in an investigation in which high achievers in high school were found vehemently to deny responsibility for their own inadequate behavior ($\underline{E}$ in the P-F) while underachievers tended (though not significantly) to admit guilt but claim that circumstances beyond their control were responsible ($\underline{I}$ in the P-F) for what had happened (Shaw and Black, 1960). Additional corroboration is found in research concerning achievement across all grades from elementary school through high school (Roth and Puri, 1967). Male underachievers, in contrast to achievers, here showed a consistent pattern—lower E-A and higher I-A and M-A. Female underachievers showed this pattern only in the sixth grade.

One contrary finding has been reported (Adler, 1964). Ninth-grade low achievers were shown to have significantly elevated extraggression and lower intraggression (especially intropunitive superego) scores than high achievers. The sample investigated, however, was extremely gifted to begin with, and therefore subject to different social pressures. For example, the highly gifted youngster who is not achieving may be unable or unwilling to accept his inferior intellectual status and channel his capacities into technical or vocational areas; he may instead resort to acting out his frustration (high E-A) as a way of standing out from the crowd. Such a youngster may also be rebelling against pressures to achieve that are exerted by parents and teachers. It should also be recognized that the above inconsistency could be due to a difference in the instruments used to define level of ability (Primary Mental Abilities Test and Cooperative School and College Ability Tests, respectively).

In general, it would appear that the outwardly energized individual displays a higher level of achievement than one who readily accepts the blame for life's frustrations. Further research on the effect of specific frustrater situations (adult versus peer) might be rewarding in this area.

Mental Retardation

The results obtained from P-F research with mentally retarded individuals have varied according to the setting (institution or school) in which testing takes place, the age of the subject and the concomitant form of the P-F (child or adult) employed, and the type of P-F administration (oral versus written) utilized.

An investigation of 102 mentally retarded public school children, aged six to 13, brought out significant differences from the normal similar to those reported with problem children; retarded youngsters displayed higher E-A and lower I-A than normals (Angelino and Shedd, 1956). The authors concluded that their retarded subjects were delayed in socialization, as reflected in P-F scores, about one age group (two years) behind the norms. In an investigation of 30 black and 30 white institutionalized children, Portnoy and Stacey (1954) reported that both groups displayed significantly higher M-A and N-P scores and lower E-D scores than those of Rosenzweig's normative sample. Analysis of P-F trends revealed that both groups tended away from E-A and toward M-A and O-D. The seeming incompatibility of these results with those of the previous investigation are probably due to situational factors. Institutionalized children are usually rewarded for inhibiting outward aggression and behaving in a docile and manageable way. Retarded children in normal settings, however, tend to imitate their normal peers in displaying outward aggression, though with some delay in inhibition relative to (intelligent) socialization. It may also be that exceptional aggressiveness is necessary for the retarded individual to "make it" in the normal world. Support for these hypotheses comes from an investigation in which no significant differences were found in the P-F responses of retardates in special education classes as compared with normal children in the same grade (Ross, 1965). However, retardates in regular classes had significantly higher E-A scores than retardates in special classes.

Some investigators have attempted to use the P-F to distinguish retarded subjects with behavior problems (children, adolescents, and adults) from well-behaved subjects in institutional settings (Lipman, 1959; Foreman, 1962). No significant P-F category or trend differences were found in this work. In fact, Foreman found that behavior-problem subjects had a lower frequency of E-A responses than "behavior models." However, both investigators used an oral administration of the P-F (which discourages E-A). Furthermore, similar difficulties, in terms of social desirability and level of behavior, exist in these investigations as in the previously discussed work on criminals and delinquents. A final difficulty that may be mentioned is that subjects of varying ages (adolescent through adult) were examined in these investigations: the children's form of the P-F (Lipman) versus the adult form (Foreman). The decision as to which form of the P-F is appropriate in research with retardates of varying ages needs to be systematically investigated.

A good example of the application of the P-F in research on mental retardation is afforded by Dunlap (1969). She found that P-F scores were significantly related to success in occupational training in a group of retarded adolescents. These adolescents had lower GCR scores than normals but these scores correlated with rating-scale scores on Adjustment, Work Quality, Personality, and Performance. Imaggression and need-persistence were also found to be significantly related to aspects of work quality and performance. Those retardates who showed the best social adjustment and ability to channel their frustrations in constructive, goal-directed ways did best in occupational training.

Reading Disability

The children's form of the P-F has been used extensively in work with retarded readers, and P-F findings have been helpful in such diagnostic and remedial efforts. Spache (1954, 1957) found highly significant ($p < .01$) P-F differences between nonreaders and normals; nonreaders exhibited increased extraggression and ego- or etho-defense and decreased intraggression. Dyslexic children have likewise been shown to be less intraggressive than their normal counterparts (Connolly, 1969), and in third-grade pupils I-A percent has been demonstrated to correlate with reading ability (Zimet, Rose, and Camp, 1973). Significant correlations have also been obtained between GCR scores and achievement in word recognition (Bishop, 1972). Retarded readers are apt to be more negativistic toward authority figures and, in general, are more aggressive than normal readers and less able to accept blame.

Speech Dysfunction

Most of the application of the P-F in the area of speech dysfunction has centered on the investigation of stuttering. Madison and Norman (1952) administered the P-F to a group of 25 adult stutterers (age 14 to 59) and found that the total group displayed significantly lower E-A and O-D scores and higher I-A and N-P scores than Rosenzweig's normative group. These findings seemed to confirm the psychoanalytic view that stuttering is compulsive in nature and involves a turning inward of aggression. However, a reanalysis of the authors' data in our laboratory discloses that P-F scores varied significantly with age. The fact that these subjects were tested anonymously also tends to diminish comparability with the normative data. These doubts are reinforced by the results of Murphy (1953), which contradicted those of Madison and Norman. His stutterers showed more E-A and less I-A than a matched control group. In general, the majority of P-F research in this area has revealed no significant and consistent differences between stutterers and matched control or normative groups (Lowinger, 1952; Quarrington, 1953; Emerick, 1967). Sheehan (1958), in a review of the P-F and other projective methods used in the investigation of stutterers, concluded that "no consistent personality pattern could be found for stutterers" (p. 24).

Courts and Prisons

The P-F has been widely employed in attempts to distinguish criminals and delinquents from normal individuals. However, group differentiation in this context depends heavily on the theoretical constructs inherent in the P-F Study. For this reason the use of the P-F in court and prison settings was discussed under primary or, more specifically, criterion-related validity. The pragmatic implications should be clear from that discussion.

Hospitals and Clinics

Psychiatric Disorders

The P-F Study has been found to have some utility in distinguishing various psychiatric groups from each other and from normals. In an unpublished investigation of normals, neurotics, and psychotics, Rosenzweig (1952) obtained tentative results which indicated that low extraggression and high intraggression in females, high imaggression in males, and high need-persistence in both sexes tend to accompany personality disturbance. The P-F was also found to be the most discriminating technique in a battery, including the Rorschach and Wechsler-Bellevue, used to investigate 36 anxiety neurotics and 36 paranoid schizophrenics (Starer, 1952). Schizophrenics exhibited significantly higher E-A scores and lower N-P and GCR scores than neurotics. Abrams (1953) observed no significant P-F differences between psychiatric patients and normals, but Diamond (1955) reported that the GCR could discriminate between psychotic and nonpsychotic individuals. Although further questions about the clinical utility of the P-F in aiding psychiatric diagnosis were raised by Brown and Lacey (1954), significant differences in E-A, I-A, E-D, N-P, and GCR scores between schizophrenics and normals were again found by Delay, Pichot, and Perse (1955). A recent effort to increase P-F predictive capacity involves the use of indices based on the relationships between P-F factors (Rauchfleisch, 1971). By these indices it was possible to discover significant differences between a group of normal subjects and two groups of neurotics. In an overview of the clinical use of the P-F, Schöfer and Meyer (1976) reported that deviations in E-A (a decrease) and I-A (an increase) are "general for being sick" while deviations in factors M' and I are "specific for a disease."

In a comparison of child-guidance patients with normals, patients were shown to have higher extraggression and lower intraggression scores at every age level along with lowered GCR scores (Rosenzweig and Rosenzweig, 1952). These results, though concerned with clinical referrals, are obviously more behavioral (or dynamic) than psychiatric-diagnostic in orientation and implication. For that reason, perhaps, the findings of this investigation are more readily intelligible and acceptable in P-F construct terms.

Suicide

From both a psychodynamic and a cultural standpoint the suicidal individual is assumed to be one who has turned aggression back on himself. It has hence been anticipated that such an individual is less apt to express hostility externally or to persist toward the solution of problems. On these assumptions attempts have been made to utilize the P-F to differentiate between normal and suicidal persons.

A first consideration in regard to suicide is the seriousness of the attempt. Farberow (1950) found that individuals who had made serious attempts on their life showed significantly less outwardly directed aggression (E-A) than individuals whose threats to destroy themselves were not judged to be genuine. Attempters also showed increased imaggression and some tendency to direct hostility inward, though mitigated by excuses (1). Recent investigators (Arneson and Feldman, 1968), however, reported that P-F category scores did not differentiate between "mild" attempters and "serious" attempters, but that mild attempters, as compared with the normative data, showed significantly higher E-D and lower O-D scores.

A second aspect in potential suicide assessment is the time and situation in which testing takes place. In an early study, Winfield and Sparer (1953) found a suicidal group of 26 patients to be less extraggressive and more imaggressive than Rosenzweig's normative group. Intraggressive tendencies were hypothesized but not found. Clinically depressed women who were given shock treatments to lift their depression were shown to have significantly higher E-A and lower I-A scores after treatment as compared with before (Bulato, 1961). An increase in GCR and need-persistence has also been reported in suicide attempters one month following their attempt as compared with the morning after (Selkin and Morris, 1971). However, when a suicidal-patient group was compared with psychiatric-nonsuicidal patients and adolescent normals, no expected differences in intraggression materialized (Levenson and Neuringer, 1970). After having reviewed some of the preceding inconsistent results, Lester (1970) concluded that the P-F "is of little use in the identification of suicidal risk."

The conflicting results concerning aggressiveness (especially intraggression) and suicide at least reflect a lack of comparability between investigations in regard to variable times at which subjects are tested, degree of seriousness of the attempt, and adequacy (in terms of matching) of control and normative samples. Recently Waugh (1974) has questioned the validity of treating suicide attempters as a homogeneous group. He found that only when attempters were divided into three suicidal-personality types did significant P-F differences in direction of aggression appear between attempters and nonattempters. Research of this nature, which goes beyond the simplistic, intraggressive stereotype of the suicidal individual, may be the key to demonstrating differences between attempters and normals.

Psychosomatic Problems

A number of studies have been devoted to the P-F results of individuals with differing psychosomatic complaints. No significant differences were observed among patients with a duodenal ulcer, essential hypertension, and neuromuscular tension (Lewinsohn, 1956) or between a group of patients with coronary artery disease and a matched group of normals (Mordkoff and Golas, 1968). However, Tridenti, Ragionieri, Rigamonti, and de Risio (1972) found that ulcerative patients, as compared with normals, showed increased intraggression and need-persistence and decreased extraggression and group conformity.

The P-F has also given support to the theory that patients with circumscribed neurodermatitis have punitive superegos and tend to express aggressiveness masochistically; these patients displayed significantly higher intropunitive superego scores ·than control groups (Seitz, Gosman, and Craton, 1953). In a related investigation, Kamiya (1959) found that leprous inpatients and outpatients had P-F scores which significantly differed from each other and from the Japanese norms. A classification of leprous patients—"resigned" and "aggressive" —was also developed in P-F terms.

P-F findings with diabetics have been mixed. Diabetic children were shown to be significantly more extraggressive and obstacle-dominant and less imaggressive, etho-defensive, and group conforming than Rosenzweig's normative group (Johannsen and Bennett, 1955). In a more recent report the P-F did not differentiate between diabetic children under good and poor control respectively, although the diabetics as a group exhibited significantly less etho-defense than the normative sample (Koski, 1969).

Some basis for differentiating pulmonary conditions by P-F results has been found. Pulmonary tuberculosis patients were reported to exhibit significantly lower GCR scores than a nondisabled control group and higher I-A scores than both an orthopedically disabled group and the control group (Adar, 1971). Later work with tubercular patients has indicated that such individuals tend to be more etho-defensive and less obstacle-dominant than normals (Vieira, Machado, de Oliveira Pereira, and Litman, 1973). Attempts have also been made to develop P-F profiles of asthmatics. When P-F scores of asthmatics, psychoneurotics, and healthy normals were compared, the asthmatics showed less extraggression and more imaggression than healthy subjects (Jores and von Kerékjártó, 1967; Pierloot and Van Roy, 1969). Insignificant differences were found between asthmatics and neurotics. More recent investigators have shown that asthmatics tend to turn aggression inward (high I-A), but significant differences between "allergic" and "nonallergic" subjects were not demonstrated (Koninckx and Dongier, 1970; Knoblach, 1971).

Alcoholism and Drug Addiction

Various researchers have attempted to develop a P-F pattern for alcoholics. Syme (1957) reported no conclusive evidence for an alcoholic-personality type in his survey of previous research. However, Murphy (1956) showed that lower-class alcoholics received significantly lower GCR and higher N-P scores than normals. Alcoholics here also scored significantly lower than the norms on obstacle-dominance. These findings in respect to obstacle-dominance and need-persistence were confirmed in a recent investigation of 44 alcoholics and 38 nonalcoholics (Coché, 1974). GCR differences did not reach significance but these scores tended to be lower than the mean for normals.

Frustration reactions of drug users have also been explored. The P-F responses of 30 heavy psychedelic drug users were compared with a matched control group (Edwards, Bloom, and Cohen, 1969). Drug dependency was found to be positively correlated with O-D, negatively with E-A, N-P, and GCR. In a project concerning marijuana use, Cormier, Bourassa, and Landreville (1973) demonstrated that group conformity ratings were significantly lower for users than for nonusers. The nonconformity of users appeared even though no significant group differences were found in any of the category scores.

The P-F has thus been shown to have variable utility in distinguishing between normals and individuals with clinical disorders. The P-F profiles of neurotics tend to differ from those of psychotics in categories E-A, I-A, N-P, and GCR. Inconsistent P-F results with suicide attempters can be attributed more to faulty methodology than to a lack of P-F validity. Application of the P-F to the area of psychosomatic illness may chiefly reflect the complexity of the area, yet tentative P-F profiles for pulmonary disease and asthma have been reported. The P-F has proved useful in the area of alcoholism and drug addiction; addicted individuals have obtained lower N-P and GCR scores than normals.

However, while some general P-F patterns of disordered behavior are apparent, it should be remembered that idiodynamic styles of behavioral pathology, as manifested in elevated or depressed category scores, may be lost in the process of examining group averages.

Cultures

Prejudice and Authoritarianism

Investigators have used the P-F to determine the types of reactions to frustration encountered in authoritarian individuals. A broad examination of authoritarianism was undertaken by Getzels and Guba (1955). They administered a number of personality measures to air force instructors who had been rated either high or low in conflict over their teacher-and-officer roles. The high-conflict group was significantly more authoritarian and had significantly higher extraggression and lower intraggression and imaggression scores on the P-F than the low-conflict group. Similar relationships between authoritarianism and extraggression scores on the P-F have been reported (Trapp, 1959; Canter and Shoemaker, 1960). In an investigation along a related dimension, Wilson (1973) compared the results of 91 subjects on the P-F and a conservatism scale. Need-persistence showed significant negative correlation with conservatism, a finding which suggested to him that conservatives lack self-reliance and prefer external control. Extraggression correlated positively with realistic, tough-minded attitudes while etho-defense correlated with ethnocentrism. These results seemed to indicate that individuals who make scapegoats of others may do so in an attempt to preserve self-respect.

Interethnic Research

The P-F has been used to examine whether different frustration-reaction patterns exist for individuals of different racial groups living in dissimilar areas of the same country. McCary (1950) administered the P-F to black and white students in northern and southern high schools. The northern group as a whole showed significantly more extraggression and less intraggression than the southern group. When the scores for the total black group were compared to those of whites, the former were found to show significantly lower I-A and a tendency toward higher E-A. P-F scores for southern black males as compared with southern white males, however, revealed a reverse pattern; blacks were less extraggressive and more intraggressive. A later examination of the P-F scores of southern black males (in 1961 as compared to 1947) showed a significant increase in extraggression and decrease in imaggression over that time period (Corke, 1962). A present-day comparison of the same sort might be quite revealing and is recommended.

Cross-Cultural Research

Hawaiian boys have been found to be significantly more extraggressive and less intraggressive and etho-defensive than their American mainland peers (Lyon and Vinacke, 1955). Similarly, Finnish children were shown to have significantly higher E-A and lower I-A and M-A scores than American children (Takala and Takala, 1957). Pareek (1958c) used standardization and normative data to compare children in American and Japanese cultures with his Indian sample. He found that Indian children were, in approximate terms, more extraggressive and less intraggressive than American children, while, as compared to the latter, Japanese children were even more intraggressive and less extraggressive. The P-F has also been used to examine assumptions concerning the passivity and/or emotional "hot temper" of Latin-Americans. No significant differences were discovered in P-F results for Guatemalan children as compared to the American norms (Adinolfi, Watson, and Klein, 1973). More intensive developmental research along these lines should prove to be illuminating.

Some research has examined the relationship of frustration reactions to social and moral development. In an East African investigation, Ainsworth and Ainsworth (1962) demonstrated that acculturation leads to increased acceptance of blame (I-A) and desire for problem solution (N-P), and decreased evasion of frustration (M-A) and emphasis on frustrating barriers (O-D). The moral values of 150 British working adolescents were explored through the use of the P-F and other projective techniques along with directed questions (Eppel and Eppel, 1966). Responses on the P-F indicated that general British level of extraggression was significantly higher than the American norms. However, since an anonymous mode of administration (which encourages E-A responses) was used it is hard to tell whether such a cross-cultural difference exists or is merely an artifact of test procedure. An item analysis according to direction of aggression revealed that most E-A was forthcoming in situations involving direct character accusation (an area in which adolescents are likely to be sensitive), most I-A was forthcoming in a situation involving property damage, and most M-A was forthcoming in situations involving being let down by a friend. On these and other bases, Eppel and Eppel concluded that the British adolescent highly values good human relations, especially in regard to loyalty and honesty, while expressing a need to be treated with respect and consideration by others.

CONCLUSION

The P-F Study has some significant relationships with various psychometric tests. Prediction based on global utilization of P-F data in conjunction with other test results (as in successive clinical predictions) tends to be more valid than that based on single-category scores. Contradictory and inconclusive P-F findings on felons and delinquents have been reviewed. Possible bases for such confusion have been offered and suggestions made for methodologically more sound research which would probe subject motivation and consequent level of response. Culturally expected differences in aggression for males and females are apparent only on the adolescent form of the P-F. During childhood and adulthood both sexes show similar patterns of reaction to frustration.

Extraggression, intraggression, imaggression, need-persistence, and GCR have been shown to be related to specific validating criteria. Ego- or etho-defense is a valid category but more research on it is desirable. The low frequency of obstacle-dominant responses has made it difficult to relate this category significantly to validating criteria. However, obstacle-dominance has been shown to be a useful construct for interpretation of global patterns of reaction to frustration.

The P-F has been pragmatically applied to a wide variety of social settings. The most frequent P-F use has been as a screening or selection device based on category and GCR scores. As such, the P-F has proved useful in business and industry, schools, and culture research. In these settings the secondary validity of directions of aggression and the GCR have been demonstrated. The categories etho-defense and need-persistence have also been shown to have differentiating potential, and some positive results have been obtained for obstacle-dominance. P-F results in hospital and clinic settings are mixed and an exclusive reliance on the P-F as a symptom-differentiating tool in such settings is not recommended. But used in conjunction with other tests or as part of a configuration index, the P-F has significant potential.

In most pragmatic research the negative aspects of aggression are emphasized under directions of aggression, especially extraggression. As a complementary approach in secondary investigations and as a means of developing additional primary support, more emphasis should be placed on the positive, constructive nature of aggression as reflected by types of aggression, especially need-persistence.

Part Two   History and Research Guide

5   Historical Conspectus

Beginning in 1928, the writer became interested in the psychology of philosophers (Schopenhauer, Nietzsche, Bergson) as focused on the interrelationships of personal frustrations, needs, and creative productions. (*Rosenzweig, 1929*). This interest led naturally to a concern with psychoanalysis (Freud, Adler, Jung), first in its application to the philosophies under scrutiny, but soon afterward in an attempt experimentally to validate the clinically derived concepts of Freud (experimental psychoanalysis). Laboratory investigations of repression, displacement, and projection (Rosenzweig, 1937; 1938c) threw into relief the phenomena of frustration as best epitomizing the psychodynamic approach in its experimental implications. In a subsequent APA symposium on frustration, clarification of these concepts was achieved from the standpoint of several investigative avenues, and it was there that this author introduced the construct of frustration tolerance (Rosenzweig, Mowrer, Haslerud, Curtis, and Barker, 1938). In brief, a psychoanalytic psychology of philosophic formulations via the biography and life experience of the formulators instigated an experimental attack on the concepts of psychoanalysis itself and, finally, produced a tentative formulation of frustration theory as an experimentally oriented psychodynamic schema.

Against this background it will be helpful to look at both the early and the later empirical formulations from which the scoring constructs of the P-F Study evolved.

In the experimental research on psychoanalytic concepts in which frustration was employed operationally to create unpleasant laboratory situations for studying memory (repression), the three ego-defensive directions of aggression (extrapunitive, intropunitive, impunitive) emerged from incidental observation in a heuristic formulation (Rosenzweig, 1934b). The following year this formulation was verified and refined in a behavioral test of reactions to frustration (Rosenzweig, 1935). The program of investigation on repression during the 1930s also produced the distinction between ego-defense and need-persistence, defined in the experiment published in 1943. The three types of aggression were thus added to the three directions of aggression and, taken together, these provided the basic scoring categories of the P-F. However, the type of aggression termed obstacle-dominance was not conceptualized until the P-F itself had been created and was being clinically explored. It was during this period that the nine factors (combining the six interrelated categories) were defined and began to serve as the scoring rubrics of the P-F. At first the relationships between the directions and the types of aggression were not fully perceived; in fact, the types were in the beginning called "types of reaction". It was not until the 1960s that both the types and directions were conceptualized as aggression and seen clearly in their interrelationships—a recognition which by gradual steps created the chart of scoring constructs presented in its definitive form in Table 1. The construct validity of the P-F rests to a considerable extent upon the experimental research here epitomized.

But while these developments with reference to the content of psychodynamics were transpiring, the formal side of the original philosophical problem was being expressed in studies of the techniques later dubbed "projective". Exploration of word association (as in the previously mentioned investigations of projection), the Rorschach method, and the just-emerging TAT paved the way for the assessment of types of reaction to frustration and of frustration tolerance by a projective device—the present P-F Study. In its earliest form (Rosenzweig and Sarason, 1942) this technique was part of a battery known as the F-Reaction Study, consisting of four parts. The first was a version of the above-cited behavioral test (Part B). Then came two questionnaires or "optionaries" (listing for each item several options of typical response together with a free space) devoted to the subject's conception of what he thought he was likely to say in frustrating situations (Part R—real response), and what he would like to think of himself as saying in such situations (Part I—ideal response). This distinction between R and I had previously been delineated by the author as a suggestion for augmenting the validity of questionnaires (Rosenzweig, 1934a). The fourth part of the battery (Part P—projective response) was the immediate forerunner of the present P-F Study. Cartoonlike drawings were employed as unstructured pictorial stimuli to elicit the subject's first associations when given the set: What would these anonymous characters say in the pictured (frustrating) situations? It will be noted that this F-Reaction

Study, as part of which the P-F first originated, posited as its organizing basis four coexistent levels of response, levels that reappeared in subsequent P-F research. But during the early 1940s the results for Part P proved to be the most fruitful and became so preeminent that the other three parts of the battery were, for the time being, abandoned. The P-F Study was thus singled out for further development. Part P of the F-Reaction Study (the present P-F Study) was first systematically highlighted in an investigation of the "triadic hypothesis" (Rosenzweig, 1938c), a hypothesis relating susceptibility to hypnosis, as a personality trait, to preferred mechanisms of ego-defense, on the one hand, and to modes of immediate reaction to frustration, on the other. The results of this work appeared four years later (Rosenzweig and Sarason, 1942).

In 1944 an outline of frustration theory as it had by now crystallized was published (Rosenzweig, 1944). In the same year there appeared the first edition of the P-F Study, adult form. At this time the earliest description of the technique appeared (Rosenzweig, Bundas, Lumry, and Davidson, 1944) and, immediately thereafter, the basic article describing the picture-association method with special reference to the assessment of reactions to frustration (Rosenzweig, 1945). The first scoring samples were published the next year (Rosenzweig, Clarke, Garfield, and Lehndorff, 1946). In 1947–48 a revised adult manual was published (Rosenzweig, Fleming, and Clarke, 1947) and three years later, a more definitive one appeared (Rosenzweig, 1950g). At this time the form for children, which had been devised and constructed during the four preceding years, was introduced (Rosenzweig, Fleming, and Rosenzweig, 1948). The present children's manual was issued in 1977 (Rosenzweig, 1977a). Research on the adolescent adaptation began in 1960 and the final revised version of the examination blank appeared in 1964. The investigation of projective distance (Bell and Rosenzweig, 1965) paved the way for the standardization of this form, and other contributions to that end followed (Rosenzweig and Braun, 1970; Rosenzweig, 1970a). Thus by 1970 versions of the P-F were available for children, adolescents, and adults.

The concluding event was the appearance of the *Basic Manual* (1978a). This comprehends all three forms (for adults, adolescents and children) with respect to the fundamental ideas and facts that they share in common. A Supplement for the adult form (Rosenzweig, 1978b) provides particulars for that level: standardization, scoring samples, group norms for categories, factors and GCR, and illustrative protocols. Comparable supplements for the other two levels are in preparation to supersede the presently available manuals for adolescents and children.

Foreign adaptations, fully standardized, were developed through close collaboration between psychologists of the respective countries and this writer, author of the original English version. As a result there became available, for use in the several countries and for cross-cultural, comparative research, versions of the P-F specifically standardized for the United States, France, Germany, Italy, Sweden, Japan, India, and for Spanish and Portuguese subjects.*

On the basis of the foregoing background it will be evident that the P-F Study was not in the first instance designed as a clinical tool, but as a method for exploring concepts of frustration theory and examining some dimensions of projective methodology. Such conceptual validity as the instrument possesses derives largely from this provenance. But the clinical, forensic, industrial, educational, and cultural applications of the instrument soon became apparent. These applications have been surveyed in Chapter 4.

---

*The citations for these foreign adaptations are given in the note on page 9.

6 Topical Guide to Research: P-F Citation Index

Research on and with the Rosenzweig Picture-Frustration Study and its precursors, dating from 1934 to 1977, is surveyed in this chapter. Investigations concerning the original versions of the P-F in English and the parallel, standardized versions in Europe, Asia, and the Americas are covered. More than 500 articles and books are organized by topic in a Citation Index giving authors and dates. The full reference for any cited item will be found in the P-F References by Author. The available references for a given topic can thus be readily located. The major topics include basic (construct) research, reliability, validity, and pragmatic applications. These applications pertain to developmental and individual differences, clinical disorders, antisocial behavior, personnel selection, counseling and therapy, educational and school psychology, family interactions, cultural and socioeconomic differences, and experimental psychodynamics.

The Rosenzweig P-F Study grew out of theoretically oriented, experimental research which began (as noted previously) in the early 1930s. The following Guide to Research on and with the P-F thus spans a period of about 40 years. From an attempt to define experimentally the clinically derived dynamic concepts of psychoanalysis, the author of the technique formulated a theory of reactions to frustration that was based upon this research and developed with a view toward further systematic knowledge of aggressive behavior. The rubrics according to which the responses to the P-F are scored rest upon these basic constructs.

In the intervening years the clinical application of the technique advanced far beyond anything that had been originally planned or expected. The P-F itself was, at first, part of a broader battery (F-Reaction Study) of frustration-reaction measures, each attuned to one level of response (implicit, overt, or opinion) but all related to one another in the behavior of the total personality. Because the P-F, as the semiprojective portion of the full instrument, soon appeared to yield the most promising measures for clinical application as well as for further systematic research, it largely eclipsed the other sections. Standardized in the beginning for use in the United States, it gradually led to parallel instruments in many European, Asiatic, and other countries (France, Germany, Italy, Sweden, India, Japan, Brazil, Argentina). These foreign-language versions represent not merely translations from the English but completely standardized devices available with norms in the given country.

The founding of the International Society for Research on Aggression in 1972 was, in part, sparked by the availability of this cross-national instrument for a comparative investigation of types of reactions to frustration. It is therefore hoped that this guide will, in addition to its more immediate uses, facilitate the international exchange of knowledge about the universal experience of frustration and the attendant modes of aggressive response. Avowedly limited in its method of approach and in its technical validity, the P-F Study is nevertheless one of the few presently existing international psychological instruments for probing and understanding frustration tolerance and the types of aggression in human behavior.

GUIDELINES

The Guide is divided into two parts: the Topical Outline and the Citation Index. From the Topical Outline the reader can at once perceive the areas in which research involving the P-F Study has been conducted, individually and conjointly, from 1934 through 1977; more than 500 relevant articles and books have appeared during this 40-year period, and the Topical Outline was developed empirically, that is, on the basis of a detailed examination and analysis of this literature. Some of these items represent experimental research on frustration directly related to the origin and development of the P-F; others refer to the standardization of the instrument in the United States or other countries; but the vast majority are concerned with the use of the technique in pragmatic investigations for which the P-F was found to be helpful.

These articles and books are cited by author and date in the Citation Index under the appropriate heading of the Topical Outline. An item is cited more than once if the content falls under more than one heading. The full reference for any item given in the Citation Index will be found under the author's name in P-F References by Author.

The Guide has been prepared to make available to a growing number of investigators the relevant literature now scattered in hundreds of journals and books and published in various parts of the world. Research on frustration and aggression should therefore be greatly facilitated by the assistance afforded here.

TOPICAL OUTLINE

I. Basic Research and Evaluation
1. Basic papers
a. Frustration and aggression constructs—conceptual
b. Frustration constructs—experimental foundations
c. Experimental frustration tests
d. Projective test constructs
2. Manuals
3. Reviews and expositions
II. Reliability
1. Scoring
2. Retest
3. Internal consistency
a. Correlational
b. Factorial and related structural analysis
III. Validity
1. Construct
2. Criterion-related
3. Pragmatic (inferred and applied): IV through XII below
IV. Developmental and Individual Differences
1. Age
2. Sex
3. Special conditions
a. Handicapped
b. Athletics
c. Extrasensory perception
4. Other situations
V. Clinical Disorders
1. Neurotic and behavior disorders
2. Depression and suicide
3. Schizophrenia
4. Epilepsy
5. Psychosomatic problems
6. Alcoholism and drug addiction
7. Other conditions

VI. Antisocial Behavior
    1. Crime
    2. Delinquency
    3. Penal-system effects
VII. Personnel Selection and Industrial Applications
    1. Personnel
    2. Accident proneness
VIII. Counseling and Therapy
    1. Counseling—educational
    2. Psychotherapy
    3. Psychiatric treatment
    4. Behavior therapy
IX. Educational and School Psychology
    1. Teacher selection and effects
    2. Achievement
    3. Mental retardation
    4. Speech correction
    5. Reading ability and disability
    6. Intelligence
    7. Other problems
X. Family Interactions
XI. Cultural, Interethnic, and Socioeconomic Differences
    1. Ethnic
    2. Religious
    3. Lifestyle
    4. Socioeconomic
    5. Prejudice and authoritarianism
    6. Cross-cultural
XII. Experimental Psychodynamics
    1. P-F as a dependent variable
    2. Projective identification
    3. Personality dynamics
        a. Personality organization
        b. Self-concept and self-esteem
    4. Levels of behavior in psychodiagnosis
        a. Personality set or behavior level elicited
        b. Social desirability, test faking, and conformity

Most of the headings are self-explanatory but a few words regarding the less obvious ones will be useful. The items cited in the first section (I) represent basic research, experimental or clinical, from which the P-F emerged. Anyone interested in the provenance of the instrument will find relevant material here, but the main purpose of these contributions is to provide an understanding of the operations through which the constructs employed in the P-F Study were derived. "Experimental Psychodynamics" (XII) includes under its first subheading ("P-F as a dependent variable") investigations in which the P-F was used before and after some experimental intervention which, it was assumed, would be reflected in the second administration. The subheading "Projective identification" deals with research in which the effort has been made to evaluate the use of pictures and captions. The subheading "Levels of behavior in psychodiagnosis" is concerned with the various degrees of consciousness (and censorship) which the subject brings into the examining situation. The discrimination among these levels (opinion, overt, implicit) was formulated by Rosenzweig (1950b) on the basis of investigative experience with the P-F.

Citation Index

I. Basic Research and Evaluation
1. Basic papers
   a. Frustration and aggression constructs—conceptual
      Rosenzweig, 1934b, 1944, 1950a, 1960, 1962, 1964, 1969, 1970, 1977b.
   b. Frustration constructs—experimental foundations
      Heller, 1939; Popp, 1974; Rosenzweig, 1933, 1937, 1938b, 1938c, 1941, 1943; Rosenzweig and Mason, 1934; Rosenzweig et al., 1938; Rosenzweig and Sarason, 1942; Sarason and Rosenzweig, 1942.
   c. Experimental frustration tests
      Rosenzweig, 1935, 1938c, 1945, 1960, 1970b.
   d. Projective test constructs
      Rosenzweig, 1950b, 1951a, 1951b.
2. Manuals
   Banissoni et al., 1954, 1955; Bjerstedt, 1968a, 1968b; Cortada de Kohan, 1968; Duhm and Hansen, 1957; Ferracuti, 1955a, 1955b; Hayashi and Sumita, 1956, 1957; Hörmann and Moog, 1957; Kramer and Le Gat, 1970; Lebbolo, 1955; Nencini et al., 1958; Nencini and Belcecchi, 1976; Nick, 1970; Pareek, 1958b, 1959b; Pareek et al., 1968; Pareek & Rosenzweig, 1959; Pichot and Danjon, 1951; Pichot et al., 1956a, 1956b; Rauchfleisch, 1978; Rosenzweig, 1950d, 1950f, 1950g, 1967b, 1976c, 1977a, 1978a, 1978b; Rosenzweig et al., 1946, 1947, 1948; Sacco, 1955.
3. Reviews and expositions
   Anzieu, 1960; Battegay and Rauchfleisch, 1974; Bjerstedt, 1964, 1965; Carli and Ancona, 1968; Challman and Symonds, 1953;

Christiansen, 1955a, 1955b; Clarke, 1951; Coetsier, 1963; Cortada, 1960; Crenshaw et al., 1968; Davreux, 1969; Delay et al., 1955; Edelman, 1959; Hayashi, 1961; Hiltmann, 1965; Hwang, 1968; Ichitani and Hayashi, 1976; Kramer, 1958b, 1959c, 1959d, 1959e, 1960, 1963, 1965; Lehner and Kube, 1955; Lindzey, 1959; Mills, 1965; Mirmow, 1952b; Nava and Cunha, 1957b; Nemes, 1968; Nencini, 1965; Nencini and Banissoni, 1954; Pareek, 1959b, 1960a, 1964; Pichot, 1954; Pichot and Cardinet, 1955; Pitkänen, 1963; Rauchfleisch, 1978; Reid, 1951; Rosenzweig, 1950c, 1950e, 1953, 1956a, 1956b, 1960, 1962, 1964, 1965, 1967a, 1968, 1976a, 1976b, 1976c, 1977a; Rosenzweig et al., 1944; Rosenzweig and Kogan, 1949; Rosenzweig and Rosenzweig, 1975, 1976a, 1976b, 1977; Schwartz, 1957b; Semeonoff, 1976; Shimazu, 1961; Snyders, 1961; Stern, 1952, 1954; Sumita et al., 1964; Sutcliffe, 1955; Trentini, 1962; Villerbu, 1969; Watson, 1951; Werner, 1966; Wilson and Frumkin, 1968; Zubin et al., 1965.

II. Reliability
  1. Scoring
    Clarke et al., 1947; Delay et al., 1955; Mirmow, 1952b; Pareek, 1958a; Pareek and Devi, 1965; Pichot and Danjon, 1955.
  2. Retest
    Adinolfi et al., 1973; Bernard, 1949; Delay et al., 1955; Mirmow, 1952b; Pichot and Danjon, 1955; Rosenzweig, 1960; Rosenzweig et al., 1973, 1974, 1975; Sanford and Rosenstock, 1952; Schwartz, 1952; Werner, 1966.
  3. Internal consistency
    a. Correlational
      Berkun and Burdick, 1964; Cox, 1957; Sutcliffe, 1955, 1957; Taylor, 1952; Taylor and Taylor, 1951; Werner, 1966.
    b. Factorial and related structural analysis
      Hayashi and Ichitani, 1964, 1970; Hayashi et al., 1959; Ichitani, 1964, 1965a, 1965b, 1965c, 1966a, 1966b; Ichitani and Hayashi, 1976; Ichitani and Maegawa, 1968; Ichitani and Takeda, 1966, 1967; Ichitani and Uemura, 1965; Klippstein, 1972; Nencini, 1956–1958; Nencini and Misiti, 1956a; Rauchfleisch, 1971b; Schalock and MacDonald, 1966; Smith, 1961; Sumita, 1961; Sumita et al., 1964.
III. Validity
  1. Construct
    Adinolfi et al., 1973; Banik, 1964; Bell, 1949; Bennett and Jordan, 1958; Cutter, 1963; De Renzi and Gatti, 1958; Fine and Sweeney, 1968; Fisher and Hinds, 1951; French, 1950; Graine, 1957; Gross,

1965; Hanvik, 1950; Harris, 1955; Hart, 1974; Holzberg and Posner, 1951; Ichitani, 1966a, 1966b; Kaswan et al., 1960; Lerner and Murphy, 1941; Leonardi, 1973; Lesser, 1959; Levitt and Lyle, 1955; Lindzey, 1950b; Lindzey and Goldwyn, 1954; Lindzey and Tejessy, 1956; Lockwood, 1975; Ludwig, 1967, 1970, 1972; MacArthur, 1955; Mausner, 1961; Meyer and Schöfer, 1974; Mirmow, 1952b; Monosoff, 1964; Nava and Cunha, 1957a; Nencini and Misiti, 1956b; Nencini and Venier, 1966a; Palmer, 1957; Pareek, 1958d; Pareek and Kumar, 1966; Pichot, 1955; Rogers and Paul, 1959; Rosenzweig, 1959; Rosenzweig and Adelman, 1977; Rosenzweig and Mirmow, 1950; Ross et al., 1963; Saito, 1973; Schalock and MacDonald, 1966; Schwartz, 1952; Schwartz and Karlin, 1954; Seidman, 1964; Siegel et al., 1957; Smith, 1958; Takala, 1953; Takala and Takala, 1957; Trentini, 1962; Walker, 1951; Wilson, 1973.

2. Criterion-related

Albee and Goldman, 1950; Angelino and Shedd, 1955; Bennett, 1958; Brody, 1974; Coché, 1974; Delay et al., 1953, 1955; Falls and Blake, 1949; Getzels and Guba, 1955; Hart, 1974; Himmelweit and Petrie, 1951; Holzberg and Posner, 1951; Ichitani and Hayashi, 1976; Jones, 1973; Karlin and Schwartz, 1953; Kramer, 1958a; Krieger and Schwartz, 1965; Liakos et al., 1977; Lindzey and Goldwyn, 1954; Lipman, 1959; Ludwig, 1970; Masson, 1973; Megargee, 1966a, 1966b; Mehlman and Whiteman, 1955; Mirmow, 1952a, 1952b; Misiti and Ponzo, 1958; Mukerji and Debabrata, 1968; Nisenson, 1972; Norman and Kleinfeld, 1958; Pareek, 1960c; Quay and Sweetland, 1954; Rao and Ramalingaswamy, 1974; Rapaport and Marshall, 1962; Rapisarda, 1962; Rauchfleisch, 1971a, 1973, 1974; Rosenzweig, 1952, 1963; Sanford and Rosenstock, 1952; Schneider, 1974; Schwartz, 1957a; Simos, 1950; Singh et al., 1972; Swickard and Spilka, 1961; Thiesen and Meister, 1949; Trapp, 1959; Trentini, 1966, 1968; Van Dam, 1970; Wallen et al., 1964; White, 1971; Wilson, 1973; Zimet et al., 1973.

3. Pragmatic (inferred and applied)
See Sections IV–XII.

IV. Developmental and Individual Differences

1. Age

Angelino and Shedd, 1955, 1956; Banik, 1964; Cesa-Bianchi and Trentini, 1962; Coetsier and Lagae, 1961; Dussan, 1974; Ferracuti and Ricciardi, 1954; Habets, 1958; Ichitani and Uemura, 1965; Lynch and Arndt, 1973; Pareek, 1960b; Rao and Ramalingaswamy, 1974; Rauchfleisch, 1978; Rosenzweig, 1952; Rosenzweig et al., 1948; Schwartz and Kleemeier, 1965; Sharma, 1975; Stoltz and Smith, 1959; Thiesen and Meister, 1949; Zimet et al., 1973.

2. Sex

Cesa-Bianchi and Trentini, 1962; Corke, 1962; Ichitani, 1964; Lockwood, 1975; Moore and Schwartz, 1963; Oeser and Emery, 1954; Rosenzweig, 1969, 1970; Rosenzweig and Braun, 1969, 1970; Roth and Puri, 1967; Sharma, 1975; Spache, 1951; Stoltz and Smith, 1959; Wendland, 1954; Zaidi and Shafi, 1965.

3. Special conditions

   a. Handicapped

Breithaupt, 1960; Dvonch, 1968; Jervis and Haslerud, 1950; Kahn, 1951; Lange, 1959; Lynch and Arndt, 1973; Solomon, 1962; TeBeest and Dickie, 1976; Van Roy, 1954; Wallen et al., 1964; Weise, 1971.

   b. Athletics

Antonelli et al., 1964; Figler, 1976; Hanin, 1976; Hashimoto, 1961; Husman, 1955; Mastruzzo, 1964; Rapisarda and Mastruzzo, 1960a, 1960b; Riccio and Antonelli, 1962; Schneider, 1974.

   c. Extrasensory perception

Eilbert and Schmeidler, 1950; Osis and Fahler, 1965; Schmeidler, 1950, 1954; Schmeidler and McConnell, 1958.

4. Other situations

Eppel and Eppel, 1966; Ferguson, 1954; Foulds, 1958; Foulds et al., 1960; Hines, 1963; Hwang, 1969; Iannaccaro, 1962; Kojima, 1960; Kramer, 1959a, 1959b; Lebbolo, 1952; Maruyama, 1969; Matton, 1961; Mikawa and Boston, 1968; Misiti and Ponzo, 1958; Petiziol and Ricco, 1960; Ricciuti, 1951; Shapiro, 1954; Simons, 1967b; Spache, 1950; Sundgren, 1964; Tausch-Habeck, 1956; Tewari and Shukla, 1968; Tewari and Tewari, 1968; Villerbu, 1967; Wessman et al., 1960; Zuk, 1956.

V. Clinical Disorders

1. Neurotic and behavior disorders

Abrams, 1953; Canter, 1953; Coleman and Seret, 1950; Cremieux et al., 1957; Davids and Oliver, 1960; Foulds et al., 1960; Harth, 1966; Himmelweit and Petrie, 1951; Hybl and Stagner, 1952; Ichitani, 1965c; Ichitani and Hayashi, 1976; Karson and Markenson, 1973; Kupferman and Ulmer, 1964; Levine, 1976; Liakos et al., 1977; Lord, 1952; Meyer et al., 1968; Minski and Desai, 1955; Němec, 1961; Nencini, 1959; Nencini and Casini Nencini, 1957; Nencini and Riccio, 1957; Pasquet et al., 1955;

Rapisarda, 1960; Rosenzweig and Rosenzweig, 1952; Schöfer and Meyer, 1976; Simos, 1950; Singh et al., 1972; Starer, 1952; Stern, 1954; Thaller et al., 1967.

2. Depression and suicide

Arneson and Feldman, 1968; Bulato, 1961; Delay et al., 1953, 1955; Dorpat and Ripley, 1960; Farberow, 1950; Holzberg et al., 1951; Ichitani and Hayashi, 1976; Lester, 1970; Levenson and Neuringer, 1970; Nencini, 1959; Nencini et al., 1953; Pasquet et al., 1955; Preston, 1964; Sacripanti, 1958; Schöfer and Meyer, 1976; Selkin and Morris, 1971; Simos, 1950; Waugh, 1974; Winfield and Sparer, 1953; Wittenborn and Plante, 1963; Wittenborn et al., 1961.

3. Schizophrenia

Albee, 1950; Brown and Lacey, 1954; Delay et al., 1953, 1955; Diamond, 1955; Foulds et al., 1960; Hybl and Stagner, 1952; Iacono, 1955; Moss et al., 1959; Nathan, 1963; Nencini, 1959; Nencini, Misiti, and Banissoni, 1954; Pasquet et al., 1955; Schöfer and Meyer, 1976; Shakow et al., 1945; Simos, 1950; Starer, 1952; Williams, 1965.

4. Epilepsy

Canter, 1953; Landisberg, 1947; Prensky, 1958–59.

5. Psychosomatic problems

Abrams, 1953; Bell et al., 1953; Belloni et al., 1956; Bennett and Johannsen, 1954; Cobb et al., 1962; Ferracuti et al., 1953; Ferracuti and Rizzo, 1955; Ferracuti and Turillazzi, 1954; Foster, 1958; Franklin and Brozek, 1949; Funkenstein et al., 1953, 1957; Gainotti and Cianchetti, 1967; Herbert, 1965; Johannsen and Bennett, 1955; Jores and von Kerékjàrtó, 1967; Kamiya, 1959; Knoblach, 1971; Koninckx and Dongier, 1970; Korkes and Lewis, 1955; Lewinsohn, 1956; Loveland and Singer, 1959; McDonough, 1964; Meyer and Weitemeyer, 1967; Meyer et al., 1968; Minski and Desai, 1955; Mordkoff and Golas, 1968; Němec, 1961; Pflanz and von Uexküll, 1962; Pierloot and Van Roy, 1969; Prensky, 1958–59; Rapisarda and Romeo, 1965; Schöfer and Meyer, 1976; Schwartz and Kleemeier, 1965; Seitz et al., 1953; Seward et al, 1951; Solomon, 1962; Tridenti, et al., 1972; Vieira et al., 1973; Volle and Spilka, 1961; Wendland, 1954.

6. Alcoholism and drug addiction

Barberini, 1961; Bathhurst and Glatt, 1959; Brown and Lacey, 1954; Coché, 1974; Coda and Bertalot, 1962; Cormier et al., 1973; Delay et al., 1955; Diamond, 1955; Edwards et al., 1969; Gold, 1960; Haward, 1969; McGlothlin et al., 1964; Murphy, 1956; Ross et al., 1963; Syme, 1957; Takala et al., 1957.

7. Other conditions

Adar, 1971; Boyd et al., 1973; Coché, 1974; Davis, 1955; Dvonch, 1968; English, 1961; Grousset et al., 1957; Guyotat and Guillaumin, 1960; Hanvik, 1950; Holzberg and Hahn, 1952; Ichitani, 1965a; Kamiya, 1959; Koski, 1969; Matton, 1961; Mouren et al., 1957; Picard et al., 1957; Rauchfleisch, 1971b; Sopchak, 1956; Stern, 1954; Sviland, 1972; Van Roy, 1954; Wittenborn et al., 1964.

VI. Antisocial Behavior

1. Crime

Barletta Reitano and Di Nuovo, 1976; De Renzi and Gatti, 1958; Dogliani and Micheletti, 1960; Mercer and Kyriazis, 1962; Petrauskas, 1962; Rosenzweig, 1963; Wolfgang and Ferracuti, 1967.

2. Delinquency

Banik, 1964; Chorost, 1962; Duhm, 1959; Ferguson, 1954; Foreman, 1962; Foster, 1958; Foulds, 1945; Friedland, 1960; Gatling, 1950; Gold, 1960; Grygier, 1954; Hart, 1974; Hashimoto, 1961; Holzberg and Hahn, 1952; Jones, 1973; Kramer, 1958b; Lindzey and Goldwyn, 1954; Lyon and Vinacke, 1955; Megargee, 1966a, 1966b; Mitchell, 1967; Norman and Kleinfeld, 1958; Petrauskas, 1962; Purdom, 1958–59; Rauchfleisch, 1973, 1974, 1976; Rosenzweig, 1963; Shapiro, 1954; Sivanandam, 1971; Smith, 1958; Solomon, 1962; Swickard and Spilka, 1961; Teichman, 1971; Temmer, 1958; Vane, 1954; White, 1971; Wolfgang and Ferracuti, 1967.

3. Penal-system effects

Bennett and Rudoff, 1960; Fry, 1949; Hecker, 1972; Kaswan et al., 1960; Mercer and Kyriazis, 1962; Peizer, 1956; Rapaport and Marshall, 1962.

VII. Personnel Selection and Industrial Applications

1. Personnel

Boisbourdin et al., 1956; Delys and Zeghers, 1955; Dooher and Marting, 1957; DuBois and Watson, 1950; Guion and Gottier, 1965; Hedberg, 1957; Jackson, 1950; Kinslinger, 1966; Kramer, 1961; Mandell, 1957; Perczel and Perczel, 1969; Pym, 1963, 1965; Reynolds, 1972; Schwartz and Levine, 1965; Sinaiko, 1949; Van Dam, 1970.

2. Accident proneness

Harris, 1953; Heiss, 1967; Krall, 1953; McGuire, 1956; Preston, 1964.

VIII. Counseling and Therapy

1. Counseling—educational

Brody, 1974; Freidland, 1960; Harth, 1966; Hashimoto, 1961; Kupferman and Ulmer, 1964; Mensh and Mason, 1951; Whetstone, 1965.

2. Psychotherapy
Bennett and Rudoff, 1960; Davis, 1955; Hecker, 1972; Hybl and Stagner, 1952; Kramer, 1958b; Maskit, 1961; Mouren et al., 1957; Peizer, 1956; Rapaport and Marshall, 1962; Rosenzweig, 1938a, 1950a, 1968; Selkin and Morris, 1971; Temmer, 1958; Van Roy, 1954.

3. Psychiatric treatment
Carpenter, 1957; Meyer et al., 1968; Moss et al., 1958; Takala et al., 1957; Wittenborn and Plante, 1963; Wittenborn et al., 1961, 1964.

4. Behavior therapy
Dunlap, 1969; Monosoff, 1964.

IX. Educational and School Psychology
1. Teacher selection and effects
Bennett, 1958; Bjerstedt, 1967; Bjerstedt and Sundgren, 1967; Downing et al., 1965; Herbert and Turnbull, 1963; Whetstone, 1965.

2. Achievement
Adler, 1964; Davids and Oliver, 1960; Hines, 1963; Junken, 1953; Nathan, 1963; Roth and Puri, 1967; Shaw and Black, 1960; Smith, 1961; Weiner and Ader, 1965.

3. Mental retardation
Angelino and Shedd, 1956; Dunlap, 1969; Foreman, 1962; Foulds, 1945; Ichitani and Maegawa, 1968; Lipman, 1959; Petiziol and Ricco, 1960; Portnoy and Stacey, 1954; Ross, 1965; TeBeest and Dickie, 1976.

4. Speech correction
Emerick, 1967; English, 1961; Lowinger, 1952; Madison and Norman, 1952; Murphy, 1953; Němec, 1961; Quarrington, 1953; Sheehan, 1958.

5. Reading ability and disability
Bishop, 1972; Connolly, 1969; Corman, 1963–64; Lieberman, 1969; McKinley, 1958; Myklebust, 1969; Purdom, 1958–59; Spache, 1950, 1951, 1954, 1955, 1957, 1963; Zimet et al., 1973.

6. Intelligence
Angelino and Shedd, 1955; Breithaupt, 1960; Karlin and Schwartz, 1953; McCary and Tracktir, 1957; Rauchfleisch, 1974; Shaw and Black, 1960.

7. Other problems
Chorost, 1962; Harth, 1966; Jervis and Haslerud, 1950; Jones,

1973; Kahn, 1951; Lange, 1959; MacArthur, 1955; Mensh and Mason, 1951; Mintz, 1968; Pitkanen, 1969; Sears and Sherman, 1964; Simons, 1967b; Sundgren, 1964; Tewari and Gautam, 1966; Tewari and Shukla, 1968; Wright and McCary, 1969.

X. Family Interactions

Bornstein and Coleman, 1956; Chorost, 1962; Foulds, 1945; Helfant, 1952; Herbst, 1954; Hwang, 1969; Iannaccaro, 1962; Karson and Markenson, 1973; Kates, 1951; Kojima, 1960; McKinley, 1958; Maruyama, 1969; Mikawa and Boston, 1968; Musgrove, 1965; Reck et al., 1969; Saltzman, 1965; Sopchak, 1956; Teichman, 1971; Weatherly, 1966.

XI. Cultural, Interethnic, and Socioeconomic Differences

1. Ethnic

Corke, 1962; Lesser, 1958; McCary, 1950, 1956; McCary and Tracktir, 1957; Megargee, 1966; Misa, 1967; Portnoy and Stacey, 1954; Solomon, 1962; Sommer, 1954; Vinacke, 1959; Winslow and Brainerd, 1950.

2. Religious

Brown, 1965; Dreger, 1952; Godin, 1960; Kirschner et al., 1962; Parsons, 1955; Saltzman, 1965; Sarker, 1969; Weatherly, 1966; Weinstein et al., 1963.

3. Lifestyle

Coons, 1957; Eppel and Eppel, 1966; Hayes, 1949; Helfant, 1952; Herbst, 1954; Levinson, 1966; Lorioz, 1965; Masson, 1973; Misa, 1967; Miyawaki, 1958; Oeser and Emery, 1954; Ricciuti, 1951; Saito, 1973; Sarker, 1969.

4. Socioeconomic

Adinolfi et al., 1973; Coons, 1957; Downing et al., 1965; Hart, 1974; Lorioz, 1965; Parsons, 1955; Saito, 1973; Stoltz and Smith, 1959; Trentini and Muzio, 1970.

5. Prejudice and authoritarianism

Brown, 1947; Canter and Shoemaker, 1960; Getzels and Guba, 1955; Harrigan et al., 1961; Harvey, 1962; Hayes, 1949; Jones, 1973; Kuethe, 1964; Lesser, 1958; Lindzey, 1950a, 1950b; Nisenson, 1972; Roberts and Jessor, 1958; Sanford and Rosenstock, 1952; Sarnoff, 1951; Sommer, 1954; Taft, 1958; Takala and Takala, 1957; Trapp, 1959; Trentini, 1970; Wilson, 1973; Wright and Harvey, 1965.

6. Cross-cultural

Adinolfi et al., 1973; Ainsworth and Ainsworth, 1962; Ferracuti and Ricciardi, 1954; Gabriel and Herd, 1960; Herbert, 1965; Hwang, 1969; Ichitani and Hayashi, 1976; Leblanc, 1956; Lyon and Vinacke, 1955; McCary, 1950, 1956; Norman and

Kleinfeld, 1958; Oeser and Emery, 1954; Pareek, 1958c , 1960a, 1960b, 1964; Rao and Ramalingaswamy, 1974; Sanford and Rosenstock, 1952; Swickard and Spilka, 1961; Takala and Takala, 1957; Triandis and Lambert, 1961; Zaidi and Shafi, 1965.

XII. Experimental Psychodynamics
  1. P-F as a dependent variable
     Albee and Goldman, 1950; Albert, 1957; Berkun and Burdick, 1964; Canter and Shoemaker, 1960; Clark, 1946; Cutter, 1963; Diamond, 1955; Franklin and Brozek, 1949; French, 1950; Ichitani and Takeda, 1966, 1967; Kates, 1952; Lange, 1959; Leonardi, 1973; Lindzey, 1959; Lindzey and Tejessy, 1956; Loveland and Singer, 1959; McQueen and Pearson, 1959; Pitkänen, 1963; Schwartz et al., 1964; Simkins, 1961; Simons, 1967a; Taft, 1971; Taylor, 1953; Timaeus and Wolf, 1962; White, 1971; Zuk, 1956.
  2. Projective identification
     Bell and Rosenzweig, 1965; Moore and Schwartz, 1963; Nencini and Venier, 1966b; Ricciuti, 1951; Saltzman, 1965; Schwartz, 1957b; Searle, 1976; Silverstein, 1957; Sutcliffe, 1955; Wallon and Webb, 1957.
  3. Personality dynamics
     a. Personality organization
        Albert, 1957; Altrocchi et al., 1964; Barber, 1964; Barta, 1962; Břicháček and Kolářský, 1959; Bulato, 1961; Canter, 1953; Christiansen, 1959; Clark, 1946; Coleman, 1967; Croce, 1968; Edelman, 1959; Fine and Sweeney, 1968; Fisher and Hinds, 1951; Getzels and Guba, 1955; Graine, 1957; Gross, 1965; Harris, 1955; Hines, 1972; Hwang, 1969; Jenkin, 1955; Kates, 1951; Lindzey and Riecken, 1951; Magistretti, 1952; Masciocchi and Monteverdi, 1958; Maskit, 1961; Mintz, 1968; O'-Connell, 1969; Otsu, 1961; Rauchfleisch, 1973; Rosenzweig, 1937, 1938a, 1938c, 1943, 1950a, 1950f, 1951a, 1967a; Rosenzweig and Sarason, 1942; Sanford and Rosenstock, 1952; Sarason and Rosenzweig, 1942; Schill and Black, 1969; Schmeidler, 1954; Schmeidler and McConnell, 1958; Schwartz, 1952; Scott, 1976; Seidman, 1964; Shor, et al., 1966; Taft, 1971; Taylor, 1953; Trentini, 1966, 1968, 1970; Weiss and Fine, 1956; Wright and McCary, 1969; Zuckerman, 1955.
     b. Self-concept and self-esteem
        Ludwig, 1967, 1970; Mitchell, 1967; Rao and Ramalingaswamy, 1974; Roberts and Jessor, 1958; Rogers and Paul, 1959; Schill and Black, 1967; Searle, 1976; Sears and Sherman, 1964; Teichman, 1971; Zuk, 1956.

4. Levels of behavior in psychodiagnosis
   a. Personality set or behavior level elicited
   Borgatta, 1951; Coleman, 1967; Grygier, 1954; Lockwood, 1975; Ludwig, 1967, 1972; McQueen and Pearson, 1959; Megargee, 1966b; Nisenson, 1972; Rosenzweig, 1934a, 1950b, 1970b; Sanford, 1950–51; Simos, 1950; Sutcliffe, 1955; Szakács, 1968; Wallon and Webb, 1957; Wechsberg, 1951.
   b. Social desirability, test faking, and conformity
   Graine, 1957; Mitchell, 1967; Pavlovic, 1964; Rosenzweig, 1967b, 1970b; Silverstein, 1957; Trentini, 1961; Whitman and Schwartz, 1966, 1967.

Part Three   Bibliographies

P-F References by Author

References by given author are arranged chronologically; more than one for a given year are arranged alphabetically by title with the appended letters (a), (b), and so on.

Abrams, E. N. A comparison of normals and neuropsychiatric veterans on the Rosenzweig Picture-Frustration Study. *Journal of Clinical Psychology*, 1953, *9*, 24–26.

Adar, L. D. An investigation of the relationship of some aspects of frustration to pulmonary tuberculosis. *Dissertation Abstracts*, 1971, *31*, 4322B.

Adinolfi, A. A., Watson, R. I., Jr., and Klein, R. E. Aggressive reactions to frustration in urban Guatemalan children: the effects of sex and social class. *Journal of Personality and Social Psychology*, 1973, *25*, 227–233.

Adler, M. L. Differences in Bright-Low-achieving and High-achieving ninth grade pupils. *Dissertation Abstracts*, 1964, *24*, 5184.

Ainsworth, M. D., and Ainsworth, L. H. Acculturation in East Africa: 2. Frustration and aggression. *Journal of Social Psychology*, 1962, *57*, 401–407.

Albee, G. W. Patterns of aggression in psychopathology. *Journal of Consulting Psychology*, 1950, *14*, 465–468.

Albee, G. W., and Goldman, R. The Picture-Frustration Study as a predictor of overt aggression. *Journal of Projective Techniques*, 1950, *14*, 303–308.

Albert, R. S. The role of mass media and the effect of aggressive film content upon children's aggressive responses and identification of choices. *Genetic Psychology Monographs*, 1957, *55*, 221–285.

Altrocchi, J., Shrauger, S., and McLeod, M. A. Attribution of hostility to self and others by expressors, sensitizers, and repressors. *Journal of Clinical Psychology*, 1964, *20*, 233.

Angelino, H., and Shedd, C. L. Reactions to frustration among normal and superior children. *Exceptional Children*, 1955, *21*, 215–218, 229–230.

Angelino, H., and Shedd, C. L. A study of the reactions to "frustration" of a group of mentally retarded children as measured by the Rosenzweig Picture-Frustration Study. *Psychological Newsletter, New York University*, 1956, *8*, 49–54.

Antonelli, F., and Riccio, D. Il P.F.S. di Rosenzweig applicato a 50 allievi dell' I.S.E.F. *Medicina Psicosomatica*, 1959, *4*, 214–219.

Antonelli, F., Tuccimei, G., and Celli, B. Il test di Rosenzweig in 30 schermitori italiani di interesse nazionale. *Medical Journal Abstracts*, 1964, *14*, 318–326.

Anzieu, D. *Les méthodes projectives.* Paris: Presses universitaires de France (Le Psychologue, 9), 1960. See pp. 164–167.

Arneson, G., and Feldman, J. Utilization of the Rosenzweig Picture-Frustration Test to distinguish suicidal gestures from suicidal attempts. Paper presented at the First National Conference on Suicidology (Research Reports 1: Current Studies of Special Suicidal Groups), Chicago, 1968.

Banik, S. N. A study of frustration and aggression in adolescent boys. Ph.D. dissertation, University of Bristol (England), August 1964.

Banissoni, P., Misiti, R., and Nencini, R. *Guida alla siglatura del P.F. Test di Rosenzweig. Bollettino di Psicologia Applicata*, 1954, 1–3, 7–127. (Manual for the Italian version of the Rosenzweig P-F Study, Adult Form)

Banissoni, P., Misiti, R., and Nencini, R. Taratura italiana del P.F. test di Rosenzweig. *Bollettino di Psicologia e Sociologia Applicata*, 1955, 9–11, 22–57.

Barbato, Z. Il P.F.T. di Rosenzweig nelle malattie mentale. *Rivista Sperimentale di Freniatria*, 1956, *4*, 854–859.

Barber, T. X. Hypnotizability, suggestibility, and personality: V. A critical review of research findings. *Psychological Reports,* 1964, *14,* 299–320.

Barberini, E. Contributo all'identificazione di rapporti tra capacità reattive tempermentali e alcoolismo cronico attraverso il "Picture Frustration Test" (P.F.T.) di Rosenzweig e una batteria di test proiettivi. *Minerva Medico-psicologica,* 1961, *4,* 4–23.

Barletta Reitano, F., and Di Nuovo, S. Aspetti della personalità del magistrato valutati con il test di S. Rosenzweig (P.F.S.). *Atti I° Convegno Regionale dell'Associazione Nazionale Giudici per Minorenni* (Catania), 1976, 5–30.

Barta, J. A study of the concurrence of anxiety and hostility. *Dissertation Abstracts,* 1962, *23,* 3471.

Bathhurst, G. C., and Glatt, M. M. Some psychological reflections on vulnerability to alcoholism. *Psychiatrie et Neurologie* (Basel), 1959, *138,* 27–46.

Battegay, R. & Rauchfleisch, U. *Medizinische Psychologie.* Bern: Hans Huber, 1974. pp. 157–159.

Bell, A., Trosman, H., and Ross, D. The use of projective techniques in the investigation of emotional aspects of general medical disorders: Part 2. Other projective techniques and suggestions for experimental design. *Journal of Projective Techniques,* 1953, *17,* 51–60.

Bell, J. E. The case of Gregor: Psychological test data. *Rorschach Research Exchange,* 1949, *13,* 155–205.

Bell, R. B., and Rosenzweig, S. The investigation of projective distance with special reference to the Rosenzweig Picture-Frustration Study. *Journal of Projective Techniques and Personality Assessment,* 1965, *29,* 161–167.

Belloni, C., Ferracuti, F., and Rizzo, G. B. Contributo sperimentale allo studio della psicologia degli amputati. *Rivista degli Infortuni e delle Malattie Professionali* (Rome), 1956. Numero Monografico dedicato alla chirurgia traumatologica.

Bennett, C. M. The relationships between responses to pupil aggression and selected personality characteristics of student teachers. *Dissertation Abstracts,* 1958, *18,* 1335.

Bennett, C. M., and Jordan, T. E. Security-insecurity and the direction of aggressive responses to frustration. *Journal of Clinical Psychology,* 1958, *14,* 166–167.

Bennett, E. M., and Johannsen, D. E. Psychodynamics of the diabetic child. *Psychological Monographs*, 1954, *68*, No. 11 (Whole No. 382), 23 pp.

Bennett, L. A., and Rudoff, A. Changes in direction of hostility related to incarceration and treatment. *Journal of Clinical Psychology*, 1960, *16*, 408–410.

Berkun, M. M., and Burdick, H. A. Effect of preceding Rosenzweig's P-F Test with the TAT. *Journal of Clinical Psychology*, 1964, *20*, 253.

Bernard, J. The Rosenzweig Picture-Frustration Study: I. Norms, reliability and statistical evaluation. II. Interpretation. *Journal of Psychology*, 1949, *28*, 325–343.

Bishop, A. L., III. The relationship between an entering first grader's tolerance for frustration, and his achievement in word recognition. *Dissertation Abstracts*, 1972, *33*, 1965A.

Bjerstedt, Å. Assessment of interaction tendencies: three approaches. *Educational and Psychological Interactions*, 1964 (Malmo, Sweden: University of Malmo, School of Education). No. 2, 1–13.

Bjerstedt, Å. The Rosenzweig Picture-Frustration Study: a critical review. In O. Buros (Ed.), *The sixth mental measurements yearbook.* Highland Park, N.J.: Gryphon Press, 1965, pp. 509–516.

Bjerstedt, Å. Interaction-oriented approaches to the assessment of student teachers. *Journal of Teacher Education*, 1967, *18*, 339–357.

Bjerstedt, Å. Rosenzweig Picture-Frustration Study: Barnversionen, svensk bearbetning. Stockholm: Skandinaviska Testförlaget, 1968. (Manual for the Swedish Version of the Rosenzweig P-F Study, Children's Form) (a)

Bjerstedt, Å. Rosenzweig Picture-Frustration Study: Vuxenversionen, svensk bearbetning. Stockholm: Skandinaviska Testförlaget, 1968. (Manual for the Swedish version of the Rosenzweig P-F Study, Adult Form.) (b)

Bjerstedt, Å., and Sundgren, P. Teacher personality and teacher effectiveness. *Educational and Psychological Interactions* (Malmo, Sweden: University of Malmo, School of Education, 1967, No. 20.

Boisbourdin, A., Michel, A., and Peltier, J. R. Experimentation du Test P. F. de Rosenzweig sur un group d'élèves pilotes de l'armée de l'air. *Revue de Psychologie Appliquée*, 1956, *6*, 15–27.

Borgatta, E. F. An analysis of three levels of response: an approach to some relationships among dimensions of personality. *Sociometry*, 1951, *14*, 267–316.

Bornstein, F. L., and Coleman, J. C. The relationship between certain parents' attitudes toward child rearing and the direction of aggression of their young adult offspring. *Journal of Clinical Psychology*, 1956, *12*, 41–44.

Boyd, I., Yeager, M., and McMillan, M. Personality styles in the postoperative course. *Psychosomatic Medicine*, 1973, *35*, 23–40.

Breithaupt, J. F. The effects of intelligence and orthopedic handicap upon selected personality variables. *Dissertation Abstracts*, 1960, *21*, 545.

Břicháček, V., and Kolářský, A. Pokus o zjištění závislosti retence na druhu reakce ve frustrační situaci [An experiment on the dependence of memory for frustrating situations on the type of reaction shown in them]. *Ceskoslovenská Psychologie*, 1959, *3*, 126–136.

Brody, M. B. The effects of rational-emotive affective education on anxiety, self-esteem, and frustration tolerance. *Dissertation Abstracts*, 1974, *35*, 3506A.

Brown, J. F. A modification of the Rosenzweig Picture-Frustration test to study hostile interracial attitudes. *Journal of Psychology*, 1947, *24*, 247–272.

Brown, L. B. Aggression and denominational membership. *British Journal of Social and Clinical Psychology*, 1965, *4*, 175–178.

Brown, R. L., and Lacey, O. L. The diagnostic value of the Rosenzweig P-F Study. *Journal of Clinical Psychology*, 1954, *10*, 72–75.

Bulato, J. C. The direction of aggression in clinically depressed women. *Dissertation Abstracts*, 1961, *22*, 1249.

Burnham, C. A. Preliminary experiments with the Rosenzweig F(rustration)-Reaction Study. Unpublished master's thesis, Clark University (Worcester, Mass.), 1939.

Canter, F. M. Personality factors in seizure states with reference to the Rosenzweig triadic hypothesis. *Journal of Consulting Psychology*, 1953, *17*, 429–435.

Canter, F. M., and Shoemaker, R. The relationship between authoritarian attitudes and attitudes toward mental patients. *Nursing Research,* 1960, *9,* 39–41.

Carli, Renzo, and Ancona, Teresa. La dinamica dell'aggressivita' dopo stimolo filmico. *Ikon (Revue Internationale de Filmologie),* 1968, *18,* 39–51.

Carpenter, L. G., Jr. Relation of aggression in the personality to outcome with electro-convulsive shock therapy. *Journal of Genetic Psychology,* 1957, *57,* 3–22.

Cesa-Bianchi, M., and Trentini, G. A further contribution to the study of adjustment in old age. In C. Tibbitts and W. Donahue (Eds.), *Social and psychological aspects of aging. Proceedings of the Fifth International Congress of Gerontology.* New York: Columbia University Press, 1962, pp. 623–627.

Challman, R. C., and Symonds, P. M. Rosenzweig Picture-Frustration Study. In O. K. Buros (Ed.), *The fourth mental measurements yearbook.* New Brunswick, N.J.: Rutgers University Press, 1953, pp. 239–243.

Chorost, S. B. Parental child-rearing attitudes and their correlates in adolescent hostility. *Genetic Psychology Monographs,* 1962, *66,* 49–90.

Christiansen, B. Rosenzweig's billed-frustrasjonstest [Rosenzweig's Picture-Frustration Test]. *Nordisk Psykologi Monografiserie,* 1955, No. 7. (a)

Christiansen, B. *Rosenzweig's billed-frustrasjonstest.* Copenhagen: Munksgaard, 1955. (b)

Christiansen, B. The latency hypothesis: a structural approach. Chapter 7 in *Attitudes towards foreign affairs as a function of personality.* Oslo: Oslo University Press, 1959, pp. 129–147.

Clark, R. A. Aggressiveness and military training. *American Journal of Sociology,* 1946, *51,* 423–432.

Clarke, H. J. The Rosenzweig Picture-Frustration Study. In H. H. Anderson and G. L. Anderson, (Eds.), *An introduction to projective techniques.* New York: Prentice-Hall, 1951, pp. 312–323.

Clarke, H. J., Rosenzweig, S., and Fleming, E. E. The reliability of the scoring of the Rosenzweig Picture-Frustration Study. *Journal of Clinical Psychology,* 1947, *3,* 364–370.

Cobb, B., Damarin, F., Krasnoff, A., and Trunnell, J. B. Personality factors and stress in carcinoma. In W. S. Kroger (Ed.), *Psychosomatic obstetrics, gynecology and endocrinology.* Springfield, Ill.: Charles C Thomas, 1962, pp. 738–765.

Coché, E. A comparison of psychotic and alcoholic psychiatric hospital patients on the Rosenzweig Picture-Frustration Study. *Acta Psychiatrica Belgica,* 1974, *74,* 365–370.

Coda, G., and Bertalot, L. Le Test de Rosenzweig et l'aggressivité latente. Etude sur 50 alcooliques. *Le Revue de l'alcoolisme,* 1962, *8,* 239–242.

Coetsier, L. Le standardization d'un test de personnalité. *Revue de Psychologie Appliquée,* 1963, *13,* 145–170.

Coetsier, L., and Lagae, C. *Frustratie-studie, een experimentele Bijdrage tot de Jeugd psychologie.* Deinze, Belgium: Caecilia Boekhandle, 1961.

Coleman, J. C., Stimulus factors in the relation between fantasy and behavior. *Journal of Projective Techniques and Personality Assessment,* 1967, *31,* 68–73.

Coleman, J. C., with Seret, C. J. The role of hostility in fingernail biting. *Psychological Service Center Journal,* 1950, *2,* 238–244.

Connolly, C., The psychosocial adjustment of children with dyslexia. *Exceptional Children,* 1969, *36,* 126–127.

Coons, M. O. Rosenzweig differences in reaction to frustration in children of high, low and middle sociometric status. *Group Psychotherapy,* 1957, *10,* 60–63.

Corke, P. P. A comparison of frustration-aggression patterns of Negro and white southern males and females. *Dissertation Abstracts,* 1962, *22,* 2870.

Corman, J. *Le Test de Rosenzweig: etude sur 50 dyslexiques.* Nantes, France: J. Corman, 1963–64, pp. 1–40.

Cormier, D., Bourassa, M., and Landreville, I. La tolérance à la frustration et le recours à la marijuana. *Toxicomanies,* 1973, *6,* 371–383.

Cortada, N. Tests de Rosenzweig, Rotter, Machover y Allen. In *Los Tests,* de B. Székely, III tomo, 4 ed. Buenos Aires: 1960.

Cortada de Kohan, N. *Test de Frustration (P.F.T.)*. Buenos Aires: Editorial Paidos, 1968. (Manual for the Spanish version of the Rosenzweig P-F Study, Adult Form.)

Cox, F. N. The Rosenzweig Picture-Frustration Study (Child Form). *Australian Journal of Psychology*, 1957, *9*, 141–148.

Cremieux, A., Dongier, S., and Dongier, D. Résultats du test de Rosenzweig chez 120 névrosés. In *Rapport du congrès des médecins aliénistes et neurologistes de France et des pays de langue française, Bordeaux, 1956*. Paris: Masson, 1957. pp. 311–318.

Crenshaw, D. A., Bohn, S., Hoffman, M. R., Matheus, J. M. and Offenbach, G. The use of projective methods in research: 1947–1965. *Journal of Projective Techniques and Personality Assessment*, 1968, *32*, 3–9.

Croce, M. A. L'influsso dell'atteggiamento psichico dello spettatore nella dinamica dell'aggressivita' dopo stimolo filmico fisso. *Ikon*, 1968, *18*, 53–63.

Cutter, H. S. G. Aggressive response strength as a function of interference with goal-oriented responses near to and far from their goal. *Psychological Reports*, 1963, *12*, 855–861.

Davids, A., and Oliver, G. R. Fantasy aggression and learning in emotionally disturbed and normal children. *Journal of Projective Techniques*, 1960, *24*, 124–128.

Davis, D. S. An investigation of the relationship of frustration tolerance in paraplegics and degree and rate of success in rehabilitation. *Dissertation Abstracts*, 1955, *15*, 1262.

Davreux, L. Quelques réflexions sur le test de Rosenzweig. *Revue de Psychologie et des Sciences de l'Education*, 1969, *4*, 448–454.

Delay, J., Pichot, P., and Perse, J. *Méthodes psychométriques en clinique: tests mentaux et interprétation*. Paris: Masson & Cie., 1955. Chapters XII-XV in Section III.

Delay, J., Pichot, P., Perse, J., and Cohen, J. La validité des tests de personnalité en psychiatrie. IV. Etude sur un test objectif et un test projectif de frustration dans la melancolie et al schizophrenie (1). *Annales Médico-Psychologiques*, 1953, *1*, 153–174.

Delys, L., and Zeghers, J. Een onderzoek naar de prediktieve waarde van de P-F study van S. Rosenzweig in beroepsselektie [Research on the predictive value of the Rosenzweig P-F Study in professional selection]. *Revue Belge de Psychologie et de Pédagogie* (Brussels), 1955, *17*, 69–96.

De Renzi, E., and Gatti, B. La personalita sociopatica alla luce della indagine psicodiagnostica. *Archivio di Psicologia, Neurologia e Psichiatria*, 1958, *19*, 509–558.

Diamond, M. D. A comparison of the interpersonal skills of schizophrenics and drug addicts. *Dissertation Abstracts*, 1955, *15*, 1439.

Dogliani, P., and Micheletti, V. Aspetti psicologici nella diagnosi delle personalita psicopatiche. *Folia Psychiatrica*, 1960, *3*, 1–14.

Dooher, M. J., and E. Marting (Eds.), *Selection of management personnel* (2 vols). New York: American Management Association, 1957. See Vol. I, pp. 462–463.

Dorpat, T. L., and Ripley, H. S. A study of suicides in the Seattle area. *Comprehensive Psychiatry*, 1960, *1*, 349–359.

Downing, G. L., Edgar, R. W., Harris, A. J., Kornberg, L., and Storen, H. F. *The preparation of teachers for schools in culturally deprived neighborhoods* (Cooperative Research Project No. 935, The *Bridge* Project). Flushing, N.Y.: Queens College, City University of New York, 1965.

Dreger, R. M. Some personality correlates of religious attitudes as determined by projective techniques. *Psychological Monographs*, 1952, *66* (Whole No. 335).

DuBois, P. H., and Watson, R. I. The selection of patrolmen. *Journal of Applied Psychology*, 1950, *34*, 90–95.

Duhm, Erna. Die Reaktionen von Problemkindern in Rosenzweig Picture-Frustration Test. *Psychologische Rundschau*, 1959, *10*, 283–291.

Duhm, E., and Hansen, J. *Der Rosenzweig P-F Test. Form für Kinder.* Göttingen: Verlag für Psychologie, 1957. (Manual for the German version of the Rosenzweig P-F Study, Children's Form.)

Dunlap, E. L. The relationship between frustration reaction and occupational training success in a group of mentally retarded adolescents. *Dissertation Abstracts*, 1969, *30*, 1863–1864.

Dussan, R. D. Standardization of the Rosenzweig Frustration Test in the adolescent population of Bogota in the fifth and sixth years of the classical baccalaureate. *Mysterium* (Bogota, Colombia), 1974, *28*, 137–158.

Dvonch, P. Anomie and physical disability: an application of the concept of anomie to psychology of the disabled. *Dissertation Abstracts*, 1968, *29*, 478–479.

Edelman, J. An idiodynamic approach to ego-defensive behavior; an experimental study of perceptual, associative and memorial reactions to aggression. *Dissertation Abstracts*, 1959, *19*, 3021–3022 .

Edwards, A. E., Bloom, M. H., and Cohen, S. The psychedelics: love or hostility potion? *Psychological Reports*, 1969, *24*, 843–846.

Eilbert, L., and Schmeidler, G. R. A study of certain psychological factors in relation to ESP performance. *Journal of Parapsychology*, 1950, *14*, 53–74.

Emerick, L. L. An evaluation of three psychological variables in tonic and clonic stutterers and in nonstutterers. *Dissertation Abstracts*, 1967, *28*, 317A.

English, R. H. Cleft palate children compared with non-cleft palate children: a personality study. *Dissertation Abstracts*, 1961, *23*, 2622.

Eppel, E. M., and Eppel, M. *Adolescents and morality.* New York: The Humanities Press, 1966. See pp. 182–212.

Falls, R. P., and Blake, R. R. A quantitative analysis of the Picture-Frustration Study. *Journal of Personality*, 1949, *16*, 320–325.

Farberow, N. L. Personality patterns of suicidal mental hospital patients. *Genetic Psychology Monographs*, 1950, *42*, 3–79. See pp. 50–56.

Ferguson, R. G. Some developmental factors in childhood aggression. *Journal of Educational Research*, 1954, *48*, 15–27.

Ferracuti, F. *Test di Frustrazione di Rosenzweig (P-F Study), Tipo per adulti.* Manuale di siglature (Revisionato). Florence: Organizzazioni Speciali, 1955. (Manual for the Italian version of the Rosenzweig P-F Study, Adult Form, Rev.) (a)

Ferracuti, F. *Del Test P-F (Picture-Frustration) di Rosenzweig. (Il tipo per fanciulli) Manuale.* Florence: Organizzazioni Speciali, 1955. (Manual for the Italian version of the Rosenzweig P-F Study, Children's Form) (b)

Ferracuti, F., Lotti, G. & Rizzo, G. B. Contributo allo studio della psicologia del canceroso terminale. *Bolletino di Oncologia* (della Lega Italiana per la lotta contro i Tumori), 1953, *27,* No. 4, 3–53.

Ferracuti, F., and Ricciardi, S. Reazioni alla frustrazione nei vecchi. *Rivista di Gerontologia e Geriatria,* 1954, *4,* No. 3, 77–95.

Ferracuti, F., and Rizzo, G. B. Psychological patterns in terminal cancer cases. *Education and Psychology,* 1955, *2,* 27–36.

Ferracuti, F., and Turillazzi, M. S. Il Test di Frustrazione di Rosenzweig nei tubercolotici. *Archives di Psycologia, Neurologia e Psichiatria,* 1953, *14,* 227–234. (Abstracted in English in *Beihefte Schweizerische Zeitschrift fur Psychologie une ihre Anwendungen,* 1954, No. 25, 81–82.)

Figler, S. K. Aggressive response to frustration among athletes and non-athletes. *Dissertation Abstracts,* 1976, *37,* 864A.

Fine, B. J., and Sweeney, D. R. Personality traits, and situational factors, and catecholamine excretion. *Journal of Experimental Research in Personality,* 1968, *3,* 15–27.

Fisher, S., and Hinds, E. The organization of hostility controls in various personality structures. *Genetic Psychology Monographs,* 1951, *44,* 3–68.

Foreman, M. E. Predicting behavioral problems among institutionalized mental retardates. *American Journal of Mental Deficiency,* 1962, *66,* 580–588.

Foster, A. L. The relationship between EEG abnormality, some psychological factors and delinquent behavior. *Journal of Projective Techniques,* 1958, *22,* 276–280.

Foulds, G. The child-family relationship and the frustration types among mental defective juvenile delinquents. *British Journal of Medical Psychology,* 1945, *20* (Part 3), 255–260.

Foulds, G. A. Superiority-Inferiority Index in relation to frustration situation. *Journal of Clinical Psychology,* 1958, *14,* 163–166.

Foulds, G. A., Caine, T. M., and Creasy, M. A. Aspects of extra- and intropunitive expression in mental illness. *Journal of Mental Science,* 1960, *106,* 599–610.

Franklin, J. C., and Brozek, J. The Rosenzweig P-F test as a measure of frustration response in semistarvation. *Journal of Consulting Psychology*, 1949, *13*, 293–301.

French, R. L. Changes in performance on the Rosenzweig Picture-Frustration Study following experimentally induced frustration. *Journal of Consulting Psychology*, 1950, *14*, 111–115.

Friedland, D. M. Group counseling as a factor in reducing runaway behavior from an open treatment institution for delinquent and pre-delinquent boys: the evaluation of changes in frustration tolerance, self-concept, attitude toward maternal figures, attitude toward other authority and in reality testing of runaway delinquent boys. *Dissertation Abstracts*, 1960, *21*, 237–238.

Fry, F. D. A study of reactions to frustration in 236 college students and in 207 inmates of state prisons. *Journal of Psychology*, 1949, *28*, 427–438.

Funkenstein, D. H., King, S. H., and Drolette, M. Intrapunitive and extrapunitive reactions to stress and their physiological concomitants. *Journal of Nervous and Mental Disease*, 1953, *118*, 267–268.

Funkenstein, D. H., King, S. H., and Drolette, M. *Mastery of stress.* Cambridge: Harvard University Press, 1957.

Gabriel, J., and Herd, J. Culturally expected responses and the Rosenzweig P-F Test, Children's Form. *Australian Journal of Psychology*, 1960, *12*, 178–188.

Gainotti, G., and Cianchetti, C. Strutture di personalita e meccanismi psicodinamici nelle cefalee. *Rivista di Neurobiologia*, 1967, *13*, 956–963.

Gatling, F. P. Frustration reactions of delinquents using Rosenzweig's classification system. *Journal of Abnormal and Social Psychology*, 1950, *45*, 749–752.

Getzels, J. W., and Guba, E. G. Role conflict and personality. *Journal of Personality*, 1955, *24*, 74–85.

Godin, A. Un test d'animisme protecteur: correlations et implications. In *Proceedings, XVIth International Congress of Psychology, Bonn, 1960.* Amsterdam: North-Holland Publishing Company, pp. 64–65. 1960.

Gold, L. Reaction of male adolescent addicts to frustration as compared to two adolescent non-addicted groups. *Dissertation Abstracts*, 1960, *20*, 4716.

Graine, G. N. Measures of conformity as found in the Rosenzweig P-F Study and Edwards Personal Preference Schedule. *Journal of Consulting Psychology,* 1957, *21,* 300.

Gross, R. D. B. A social situations test as a measure of adjustment mechanisms. *Dissertation Abstracts,* 1965, *28,* 2137B.

Grousset, C., Picard, P., Pasquet, P., and Quero, R. Le P.F.T. et le questionnaire Cornell Index en pratique psychiatrique. *Comptes rendus du 54 Congrès des médecins aliénistes et neurologistes de France et des pays de langue française. Bordeaux, 1956.* Paris: Masson, 1958. pp. 285–293.

Grygier, T. *Oppression.* London: Kegan Paul, 1954. (The P-F study is dealt with at length in this volume; see especially Chapters III, V, VI and VIII.)

Guion, R. M., and Gottier, R. F. Validity of personality measures in personnel selection. *Personnel Psychology,* 1965, *18,* 135–164.

Guyotat, J., and Guillaumin, J. Un aspect de l'adaptation du malade à la situation morbide: L'étude des réactions d'un groupe de chirurgicaux au Test de Frustration de Rosenzweig. *Revue de Psychologie Appliquée,* 1960, *10,* 39–58.

Habets, J. J. G. M. Enige bevindingen over de Rosenzweig "Picture-Frustration Study" voor Kinderen [Some experiences with the Rosenzweig Picture-Frustration Study for Children]. *Netherlands Tijdschrift voor de Psychologie en Grensgebieden,* 1958, *13,* 205–228.

Hanin, Y. L. P-F research in sports and athletics. Leningrad Research Institute of Physical Culture, 1976. Personal communication, September 3, 1976.

Hanvik, L. J. Some comparisons and correlations between MMPI and Rosenzweig P-F Study scores in a neuropsychiatric hospital sample. *Journal of Colorado-Wyoming Academy of Science,* 1950, *4,* 70. (Abstract)

Hardesty, F. P. Discussion of Dr. Rosenzweig's paper. (See Rosenzweig [1970] on the Adolescent Form of the P-F Study.) In J. Zubin and A. Freedman (Eds.), *Psychopathology of Adolescence.* New York: Grune & Stratton, 1970, pp. 103–107.

Harrigan, J. E., Dole, A. A., and Vinacke, W. E. A study of indignation-bigotry and extrapunitiveness in Hawaii. *Journal of Social Psychology,* 1961, *55,* 105–112.

Harris, F. J. Can personality tests identify accident-prone employees? *Personnel Psychology*, 1950, *3*, 455–459. (See page 458.)

Harris, M. W. Protective mechanisms utilized in reaction to ego-threatening situations, as evidenced by performance on a level-of-aspiration problem. *Dissertation Abstracts*, 1955, *15*, 1116.

Hart, I. *Factors relating to reconviction among young Dublin probationers* (Paper No. 76). Dublin: The Economic and Social Research Institute, 1974.

Harth, R. Changing attitudes toward school, classroom behavior, and reaction to frustration of emotionally disturbed children through role playing. *Exceptional Children*, 1966, *33*, 119–120.

Harvey, O. J. Personality factors in resolution of conceptual incongruities. *Sociometry*, 1962, *25*, 336–352.

Hashimoto, S. I. Observation of "Pupil T." with a socialization problem. II. The application of the P-F to the delinquent child and for guidance of parents. III. The characteristics of children in the Basket-ball Club as measured by the P-F Study. *Psychological Test Bulletin* (Kyoto City, Japan: Sankyobo) 1961, *1*, 25–33.

Haward, L. R. C. Differential modifications of verbal aggression by psychotropic drugs. In S. Garattini and E. B. Sigg (Eds.), *Aggressive behavior.* Amsterdam: Excerpta Medica Foundation, 1969, pp. 317–321.

Hayashi, K. Rosenzweig's P-F Study. *Psychological Test Bulletin* (Kyoto City, Japan: Sankyobo) 1961, *1*, 7–18.

Hayashi, K., and Ichitani, T. Factorial, experimental and clinical study of human personality especially in terms of the Rosenzweig P-F Study and his personality theory: the factorial structure in young delinquent group and the clinical relationships of factorial types to psychopathic personality. *Bulletin of the Kyoto Gakugei University*, 1964, Ser. A., No. 25, 61–70.

Hayashi, K., and Ichitani, T. Factorial patterns of the Rosenzweig P-F Study. *Psychologia*, 1970, *13*, 181–191.

Hayashi, K., and Sumita, K. The Rosenzweig P-F Study, Children's Form. Kyoto City: Sankyobo, 1956. (Manual for the Japanese version of the Rosenzweig P-F Study, Children's Form)

Hayashi, K., and Sumita, K. The Rosenzweig P-F Study, Adult Form. Kyoto

City: Sankyobo, 1957. (Manual for the Japanese version of the Rosenzweig P-F Study, Adult Form)

Hayashi, K., Sumita, K., and Ichitani, T. A factorial study of the Rosenzweig Picture-Frustration Study. *Japanese Psychological Research,* 1959, No. 8, 20–26.

Hayes, M. L. Personality and cultural factors in intergroup attitudes: I and II. *Journal of Educational Research,* 1949, *43,* 122–128, 197–204.

Hecker, B. Frustration tolerance, aggression and intervention methods for a population of non-institutionalized offenders. *Dissertation Abstracts,* 1972, *33,* 2104A.

Hedberg, R. The Rosenzweig Picture-Frustration Study in relation to life insurance salesmen. *American Psychologist,* 1957, *12,* 408. (Abstract)

Heiss, H. W. Unfallverhütung als Aufgabe der präventiven Medizin: Ergebnis einer Untersuchung psychogener Unfallbedingungen. *Psychotherapy & Psychosomatics,* 1967, *15,* 28–29. (Abstract) (Paper presented at the 7th International Congress of Psychotherapy, Wiesbaden, 1967.)

Helfant, K. Parents' attitudes vs. adolescent hostility in the determination of adolescent sociopolitical attitudes. *Psychological Monographs,* 1952, *66* (Whole No. 345).

Heller, S. M. An experimental study of frustration in pre-school children. Unpublished master's thesis, Clark University (Worcester, Mass.) 1939.

Herbert, M. Personality factors and bronchial asthma: a study of South African Indian children. *Journal of Psychosomatic Research,* 1965, *8,* 353–364.

Herbert, N., and Turnbull, G. H. Personality factors and effective progress in teaching. *Education Review,* 1963, *16,* 24–31.

Herbst, P. G. Family living—patterns of interaction. In O. A. Oeser and S. B. Hammond (Eds)., *Social structure and personality in a city.* Studies of social behavior, Vol. 1. New York: Macmillan, 1954. See page 178.

Hiltmann, H. Wortassoziation und verbale Ergänzungsverfahren. In R. Heiss (Ed.). *Handbuch der Psychologie,* Band 6. Göttingen: Hogrefe, 1964.

Hiltmann, H. El experimento de asociacion, el diagnostico del hecho y los test de asociacion. III. El Picture-Frustration-Test de Rosenzweig. *Psicologia Industrial* (Avellaneda Argentina), 1965, *5*, 35–46.

Himmelweit, H., and Petrie, A. The measurement of personality in children: an experimental investigation of neuroticism. *British Journal of Educational Psychology*, 1951, *21*, 9–29.

Hines, M. P. The relationship of achievement level to certain personality factors among high school seniors. *Dissertation Abstracts*, 1963, *24*, 5193.

Hines, T. F. A multitrait-multimethod analysis of the internal-external control concept. *Dissertation Abstracts*, 1972, *32*, 5442B.

Holzberg, J. D., Cahen, E. R., and Wilk, E. K. Suicide: a psychological study of self-destruction. *Journal of Projective Techniques*, 1951, *15*, 339–354.

Holzberg, J. D., and Hahn, F. The Picture-Frustration technique as a measure of hostility and guilt reactions in adolescent psychopaths. *American Journal of Orthopsychiatry*, 1952, *22*, 776–795.

Holzberg, J. D., and Posner, R. The relationship of extrapunitiveness on the Rosenzweig Picture-Frustration Study to aggression in overt behavior and fantasy. *American Journal of Orthopsychiatry*, 1951, *21*, 767–779.

Hörmann, H., and Moog, W. *Der Rosenzweig P-F Test. Form für Erwachsene.* Göttingen: Verlag für Psychologie, 1957. (Manual for the German version of the Rosenzweig P-F Study, Adult Form)

Husman, B. F. Aggression in boxers and wrestlers as measured by projective techniques. *Research Quarterly* (American Association for Health, Physical Education and Recreation), 1955, *26*, 421–425.

Hwang, C.-H. Reaction of Chinese university students to Rosenzweig's Picture-frustration Study. *Psychology and Education* (Taiwan), 1968, *2*, 37–48.

Hwang, C.-H. Parent-child resemblance in psychological characteristics. *Psychology and Education* (Taiwan), 1969, *3*, 29–36.

Hybl, A. R., and Stagner, R. Frustration tolerance in relation to diagnosis and therapy. *Journal of Consulting Psychology*, 1952, *16*, 163–170.

Iacono, G. Il reattivo di Rosenzweig nello studio dei soggetti ai limiti tra psicastenia e schizofrenia. Contributi del Laboratorio di Psicologia. *Pubblicazioni dell' Universita Cattolica del S. Cuore* (Milan), 1955, *49*, Nuova Serie, 119–126.

Iannaccaro, E. Studio dei modi di reazione alla frustrazione in funzione di certe variabili familiari in un gruppo di adolescenti. *Contributi dell'Istituto di Psicologia,* 1962, *25,* 374–387.

Ichitani, T. Factorial, experimental and clinical study of human personality especially in terms of the Rosenzweig P-F Study and his personality theory: the developmental tendencies and sex difference on factorial structure between normal boys and girls. *Bulletin of the Kyoto Gakugei University,* 1964, Ser. A., No. 25, 45–60.

Ichitani, T. Factorial, experimental and clinical study of ... Rosenzweig P-F: a differential study of within-group behaviors in playing volleyball game between the obsessive and paranoid groups as constructed in accordance with the factor scores derived from factor analysis of the P-F Study. *Bulletin of the Kyoto Gakugei University,* 1965, Ser. A., No. 26, 29–44. (a)

Ichitani, T. Factorial, experimental and clinical study of ... Rosenzweig P-F: a differential study of within-group behaviors in playing competitive games among the groups as constructed in accordance with the factor scores derived from factor analysis of the P-F Study. *Bulletin of the Kyoto Gakugei University,* 1965, Ser. A, No. 26, 45–62. (b)

Ichitani, T. Factorial, experimental and clinical study of ... Rosenzweig P-F: the factorial structure of neurotic patients. *Bulletin of the Kyoto Gakugei University,* 1965, Ser. A, No. 27, 35–46. (c)

Ichitani, T. Factorial, experimental and clinical study of ... Rosenzweig P-F: a study on the relationship between factorial types and M.P.I. *Bulletin of the Kyoto Gakugei University,* 1966, Ser. A., No. 28, 1–10. (a)

Ichitani, T. Factorial, experimental and clinical study of ... Rosenzweig P-F: an experimental study of relationships between factorial personality types and IR (reactive inhibition). *Bulletin of the Kyoto Gakugei University,* 1966, Ser. A, No. 29, 125–137. (b)

Ichitani, T., and Hayashi, K. *Basic research in projective methods focused on the Rosenzweig P-F Study.* Tokyo: Kazama Book Co., 1976. (In Japanese)

Ichitani, T., and Maegawa, Y. Responses of mentally retarded children to the Rosenzweig P-F Study and a factor analysis of them. *Bulletin of the Kyoto Gakugei University,* 1968, Ser. A, No. 32, 77–99.

Ichitani, T., and Takeda, M. Factorial, experimental and clinical study of ... Rosenzweig P-F: an experimental study of relationships between factorial personality types and I.T.P. (interruption task paradigm). *Bulletin of the Kyoto Gakugei University,* 1966, Ser. A, No. 29, 101–124.

Ichitani, T., and Takeda, M. A factor analytic study on criterion scores of interrupted task paradigm (I.T.P.). *Bulletin of the Kyoto Gakugei University,* 1967, Ser. A, No. 30, 35–45.

Ichitani, T., and Uemura, M. Factorial, experimental and clinical study of ... Rosenzweig P-F: The factorial structure of senior high school students. *Bulletin of the Kyoto Gakugei University,* 1965, Ser. A, No. 27, 23–33.

Jackson, P. Frustration tolerance in social situations as a factor in successful retail salesmanship. *Microfilm Abstracts,* 1950, *10,* 225.

Jenkin, N. Some relationships between projective test behavior and perception. *Journal of Clinical Psychology,* 1955, *11,* 278–281.

Jervis, F. M., and Haslerud, G. H. Quantitative and qualitative difference in frustration between blind and sighted adolescents. *Journal of Psychology,* 1950, *29,* 67–76.

Johannsen, D. E., and Bennett, E. M. The personality of diabetic children. *Journal of Genetic Psychology,* 1955, *87,* 175–185.

Jones, H. Approved schools and attitude change. *British Journal of Criminology,* 1973, *13,* 148–156.

Jores, A., and von Kerékjártó, M. *Der Asthmatiker: Äitologie und Therapie des Asthmas bronchiale in psychologischer Sicht.* Bern: Hans Huber, 1967. (See pp. 150f.)

Junken, E. M. A comparison of the reactions of frustration of children academically advanced with those of children academically retarded. *Dissertation Abstracts,* 1953, *13,* 583.

Kahn, H. A comparative investigation of the response to frustration of normal-hearing and hypacousic children. *Microfilm Abstracts,* 1951, *11,* 959–960.

Kamiya, M. Psychiatric studies on leprosy. *Folia Psychiatrica et Neurologica Japonica,* 1959, *13,* 143–173.

Karlin, L., and Schwartz, M. M. Social and general intelligence and performance on the Rosenzweig Picture-Frustration Study. *Journal of Consulting Psychology,* 1953, *17,* 293–296.

Karson, S., and Markenson, D. J. Some relations between parental personality factors and childhood symptomatology. *Journal of Personality Assessment,* 1973, *37,* 249–254.

Kaswan, J., Wasman, M., and Freedman, L. Z. Aggression and the Picture-Frustration Study. *Journal of Consulting Psychology,* 1960, *24,* 446–452.

Kates, S. L. Suggestibility, submission to parents and peers, and extrapunitiveness, intropunitiveness, and impunitiveness in children. *Journal of Psychology,* 1951, *31,* 233–241.

Kates, S. L. Subjects' evaluations of annoying situations after being described as well adjusted and poorly adjusted. *Journal of Consulting Psychology,* 1952, *16,* 429–434.

Kinslinger, H. J. Application of projective techniques in personnel psychology since 1940. *Psychological Bulletin,* 1966, *66,* 134–149.

Kirschner, R., McCary, J. L., and Moore, C. W. A comparison of differences among several religious groups of children on various measures of the Rosenzweig Picture-Frustration Study. *Journal of Clinical Psychology,* 1962, *18,* 352–353.

Klippstein, E. Eine Analyse der Rosenzweig P-F Test-Situationen (Form für Kinder). *Zeitschrift für Experimentelle und Angewandte Psychologie,* 1972, *19,* 444–459.

Knoblach, D. Psychogene Aspekte beim Asthma bronchiale. *Zeitschrift für Klinische Psychologie und Psychotherapie,* 1971, *19,* 163–177.

Kojima, H. Oyako kankei to yoji no shakaika [Parent-child relationship and socialization of preschool children]. *Japanese Journal of Educational Psychology,* 1960, *7,* 200–209.

Koninckx, N., and Dongier, S. Tentative d'objectivation par les tests de Rosenzweig et PNP de la composante névrotique chez 28 asthmatiques. *Acta Psychiatrica Belgica,* 1970, *70,* 610–622.

Korkes, L., and Lewis, N. D. An analysis of the relationship between psychological patterns and outcome in pulmonary tuberculosis. *Journal of Nervous and Mental Disease,* 1955, *122,* 524–563.

Koski, M.-L. The coping processes in childhood diabetes. *Acta Paediatrica Scandinavica,* Supplement (Stockholm), 1969, *198,* 1–56.

Krall, V. Personality characteristics of accident repeating children. *Journal of Abnormal and Social Psychology*, 1953, *48*, 99–107.

Kramer, C. La conformité au groupe, facteur d'adaptation sociale. *Proceedings, XIIIth Congress of Applied Psychology*, Rome, 1958, 622–623. (a)

Kramer, C. Expérimentation du Test de Frustration de Rosenzweig: travaux recents. *Revue de Psychologie Appliquée*, 1958, *8*, 153–158. (b)

Kramer, C. Carences, privations et frustration. *Enfance* (Paris), 1959, *12*, 187–190. (a)

Kramer, C. *La frustration: une étude de psychologie différentielle* (Préface par S. Rosenzweig). Neuchatel, Switzerland: Delachaux et Niestlé, 1959. (b)

Kramer, C. Les qualities metrologigues du test du Frustration de Rosenzweig. *Bulletin du Centre d'Études et Recherches Psychotechniques*, 1959, *8*, 165–167. (c)

Kramer, C. Tables des tendances et des poucentages pour le P-F test. Paris: Les Éditions du Centre de Psychologie Appliquée, 1959. (d)

Kramer, C. Le test de frustration de Rosenzweig. Expérimentation d'une épreuve projective. *Bulletin de l'Institut National d'Étude du Travail et d'Orientation Professionnelle*, 1959, 2 Série, 15 Année, 85–93. (e)

Kramer, C. Technica projectiva en clinicas psiquiatricas y en psicoterapia: P-F Test de Rosenzweig. *Revista de Psiquiatria y Psicologia Medica*, 1960, *6*, 479–480.

Kramer, C. Le Test de Rosenzweig et les réactions à la frustration. *Bulletin de Psychologie*, 1963, *17*, 338–347.

Kramer, C. Applications du Test P-F. *Revue de Psychologie Appliquée*, 1965, *15*, 70–85.

Kramer, C, and Le Gat, A. *Manuel du Test de Frustration de Rosenzweig, Forme pour Adolescents*. Paris: Les Editions du Centre de Psychologie Appliquée, 1970. (Manual for the French version of the Rosenzweig P-F Study, Adolescent Form)

Krieger, L., and Schwartz, M. M. The relationship between sociometric measures of popularity among children and their reactions to frustration. *Journal of Social Psychology*, 1965, *66*, 291–296.

Kuethe, J. L. Prejudice and aggression: a study of specific social schemata. *Perceptual and Motor Skills,* 1964, *18,* 107–115.

Kupferman, S. C., and Ulmer, R. A. An experimental total-push program for emotionally disturbed adolescents. *Personnel and Guidance Journal,* 1964, *42,* 894–898.

Landisberg, S. A personality study of institutionalized epileptics. *American Journal of Mental Deficiency,* 1947, *52,* 16–22.

Lange, Patricia. Frustration reactions of physically handicapped children. *Exceptional Children,* 1959, *25,* 355–357.

Lebbolo, F. Esame comparativo di 50 donne nubili e di 50 donne sposate col "P.F. Test" di S. Rosenzweig. Contributi del Laboratoria di Psicologia. *Pubblicanzioni dell'Universita Cattolica del S. Cuore* (Milan), 1952, *41,* Nuova Serie, 261–280.

Lebbolo, F. Contributo allo studio del "P.F. Study—Children's Form" di Saul Rosenzweig. Contributi del Laboratorio di Psicologia. *Pubblicanzioni dell' Universita Cattolica del S. Cuore* (Milan), 1955, *49,* Nuova Serie, 300–402.

Leblanc, M. Adaptation africaine et comparaison interculturelle d'une épreuve projective: Test de Rosenzweig. *Revue de Psychologie Appliquée,* 1956, *6,* 91–109.

Lehner, G. F. J., and Kube, E. *The dynamics of personal adjustment.* New York: Prentice-Hall, 1955. See pp. 95–109.

Leonardi, A. M. Differences in a generalized expectancy for internal-external locus of control and direction and type of reaction to frustration. *Dissertation Abstracts,* 1973, *33,* 6092A.

Lerner, E., and Murphy, L. B. Methods of the study of personality in young children: blocking technique Number 1. *Monographs of the Society for Research in Child Development,* 1941, *6,* Serial No. 30, 164–186.

Lesser, G. S. Extrapunitiveness and ethnic attitude. *Journal of Abnormal and Social Psychology,* 1958, *56,* 281–282.

Lesser, G. S. Population differences in construct validity. *Journal of Consulting Psychology,* 1959, *23,* 60–65.

Lester, D. Attempts to predict suicidal risk using psychological tests. *Psychological Bulletin*, 1970, *74*, 1–17.

Levenson, M., and Neuringer, C. Intropunitiveness in suicidal adolescents. *Journal of Projective Techniques and Personality Assessment*, 1970, *34*, 409–411.

Levine, B. P. Aversive conditioning and type and direction of aggression as factors influencing bruxing: a paradoxical effect. *Dissertation Abstracts*, 1976, *36*, 5762–5763.

Levinson, B. M. Subcultural studies of homeless men. *Transactions of the New York Academy of Sciences*, 1966, *29*, 165–182.

Levitt, E., and Lyle, W. H., Jr. Evidence for the validity of the Children's Form of the Picture-Frustration Study. *Journal of Consulting Psychology*, 1955, *19*, 381–386.

Lewinsohn, P. Personality correlates of duodenal ulcer and other psychosomatic reactions. *Journal of Clinical Psychology*, 1956, *12*, 296–298.

Liakos, A., Markidis, M., Kokkevi, A., and Stefanis, C. The relation of anxiety to hostility and frustration in neurotic patients. In C. D. Spielberger and I. G. Sarason (Eds.), *Stress and anxiety: IV.* Washington, D.C.: Hemisphere, 1977. pp. 291–301.

Lieberman, M. Projective responses of retarded and adequate readers to frustrating academic *vs.* nonacademic situations. *Dissertation Abstracts*, 1969, *29*, 3004A.

Lindzey, G. An experimental examination of the scapegoat theory of prejudice. *Journal of Abnormal and Social Psychology*, 1950, *45*, 296–309. (a)

Lindzey, G. An experimental test of the validity of the Rosenzweig Picture-Frustration Study. *Journal of Personality*, 1950, *18*, 315–320. (b)

Lindzey, G. On the classification of projective techniques. *Psychological Bulletin*, 1959, *56*, 158–168.

Lindzey, G., and Goldwyn, R. M. Validity of the Rosenzweig Picture-Frustration Study. *Journal of Personality*, 1954, *22*, 519–547.

Lindzey, G., and Riecken, H. W. Inducing frustration in adult subjects. *Journal of Consulting Psychology*, 1951, *15*, 18–23.

Lindzey, G., and Tejessy, C. Thematic Apperception Test: indices of aggression in relation to measures of overt and covert behavior. *American Journal of Orthopsychiatry,* 1956, *26,* 567–576.

Lipman, R. S. Some test correlates of behavioral aggression in institutionalized retardates with particular reference to the Rosenzweig Picture-Frustration Study. *American Journal of Mental Deficiency,* 1959, *63,* 1038–1045.

Lockwood, J. L. The effects of fantasy behavior, level of fantasy predisposition, and anxiety on direction of aggression in young children. *Dissertation Abstracts,* 1975, *36,* 1442B.

Lord, J. P. Psychological correlates of nocturnal enuresis in male children. Unpublished Ph.D. thesis, Harvard University, 1952. Summarized in Rosenzweig, 1960, p. 170.

Lorioz, A. Test de Rosenzweig et statut sociométrique. *Revue de Psychologie Appliquee,* 1965, *15,* 25–31.

Loveland, N. T., and Singer, M. T. Projective test assessment of the effects of sleep deprivation. *Journal of Projective Techniques,* 1959, *23,* 323–334.

Lowinger, L. The psychodynamics of stuttering: an evaluation of the factors of aggression and guilt feelings in a group of institutionalized children. *Dissertation Abstracts,* 1952, *12,* 725.

Ludwig, D. J. Levels of behavior in reaction to frustration as related to the self-concept, with special reference to the Rosenzweig F-Battery. *Dissertation Abstracts,* 1967, *27,* 4578B.

Ludwig, D. J. Evidence of construct and criterion-related validity for the self-concept. *Journal of Social Psychology,* 1970, *80,* 213–223.

Ludwig, D. J. Toward development of a projective set. *Journal of Personality Assessment,* 1972, *36,* 567–572.

Lynch, D. J., and Arndt, C. Developmental changes in response to frustration among physically handicapped children. *Journal of Personality Assessment,* 1973, *37,* 130–135.

Lyon, W., and Vinacke, W. E. Picture-Frustration Study responses of institutionalized and non-institutionalized boys in Hawaii. *Journal of Social Psychology,* 1955, *41,* 71–83.

MacArthur, R. S. An experimental investigation of persistence in secondary school boys. *Canadian Journal of Psychology*, 1955, *9*, 42–54.

McCary, J. L. Ethnic and cultural reactions to frustration. *Journal of Personality*, 1950, *18*, 321–326.

McCary, J. L. Picture-Frustration Study normative data for some cultural and racial groups. *Journal of Clinical Psychology*, 1956, *12*, 194–195.

McCary, J. L., and Tracktir, J. Relationship between intelligence and frustration-aggression patterns as shown by two racial groups. *Journal of Clinical Psychology*, 1957, *13*, 202–204.

McDonough, L. B. Inhibited aggression in essential hypertension. *Journal of Clinical Psychology*, 1964, *20*, 447.

McGlothlin, W. H., Cohen, S., and McGlothlin, M. S. Short-term effects of LSD on anxiety, attitudes, and performance. *Journal of Nervous and Mental Disease*, 1964, *139*, 266–273.

McGuire, F. L. Rosenzweig Picture-Frustration Study for selecting safe drivers. *U.S. Armed Forces Medical Journal*, 1956, *7*, 200–207.

McKinley, D. P. A study of certain relationships of maternal personality and child-rearing attitudes to children's reading performances. *Dissertation Abstracts*, 1958, *19*, 3216.

McKinney, F., Strother, G. B., Hines, R. R., and Allee, H. A. Experimental frustration in a group test situation. *Journal of Abnormal and Social Psychology*, 1951, *46*, 316–323.

McQueen, R., and Pearson, W. O. Stimulus-word changes in picture-frustration situations. *Perceptual and Motor Skills*, 1959, *9*, 407–410.

Madison, L., and Norman, R. D. A comparison of the performance of stutterers and non-stutterers on the Rosenzweig Picture-Frustration test. *Journal of Clinical Psychology*, 1952, *8*, 179–183.

Magistretti, F. Studio su alcuni aspetti della frustrazione sociale. Contributi del Laboratorio di Psicologia. Serie Decimasesta. *Pubblicazioni dell' Universita Cattolica del Sacro Cuore* (Milan), 1952, *41*, Nuova Serie, 230–260.

Mandell, M. M. How to gage executive potential. *Dun's Review*, 1957, *69*, 43–45, 95–107. See page 45.

Maruyama, Y. The sense of competence in middle adolescent boys. *Dissertation Abstracts*, 1969, *30*, 2405–2406.

Masciocchi, A., and Monteverdi, T. Considerazioni sulla memoria in rapporto alla frustrazione mediante il P.F.T. di Rosenzweig. *Archivio di Psicologia, Neurologia e Psichiatria*, 1958, *19*, 27–39.

Maskit, M. L. Management of aggression in preadolescent girls: its effect on certain aspects of ego functioning. *Dissertation Abstracts*, 1961, *22*, 917.

Masson, H. The leader in children's groups: a study of the personalities of young boys living in school: II. *Bulletin de Psychologie Scolaire et d'Orientation*, 1973, *22*, 102–147.

Mastruzzo, A. Risultati ottenuti con l'applicazione del P.F.S. di Rosenzweig in venti pugili dilettanti. *Medical Journal Abstracts*, 1964, *14*, 335–350.

Matton, D. *Le Test de Rosenzweig chez l'enfant anormal. Frustration et troubles caracteriels.* Lille, France. Impr. F. Planquart, 1961.

Mausner, B. Situational effects on a projective test. *Journal of Applied Psychology*, 1961,. *45*, 186–192.

Megargee, E. A comparison of the scores of White and Negro male juvenile delinquents on three projective tests. *Journal of Projective Techniques and Personality Assessment*, 1966, *30*, 530–535. (a)

Megargee, E. Undercontrolled and overcontrolled personality types in extreme antisocial aggression. *Psychological Monographs*, 1966, *80*, 1–29. (b)

Mehlman, B., and Whiteman, S. L. The relationship between certain pictures of the Rosenzweig Picture-Frustration Study and corresponding behavioral situations. *Journal of Clinical Psychology*, 1955, *11*, 15–19.

Mensh, I. N., and Mason, E. P. Relationship of school atmosphere to reactions in frustrating situations. *Journal of Educational Research*, 1951, *45*, 275–286.

Mercer, M., and Kyriazis, C. Results of the Rosenzweig Picture-Frustration Study for physically assaultive prisoner mental patients. *Journal of Consulting Psychology*, 1962, *26*, 490.

Meyer, A.-E., Golle, R., and Weitemeyer, W. Duration of illness and elevation of neuroticism scores. *Journal of Psychosomatic Research*, 1968, *11*, 347–355.

Meyer, A.-E., and Schöfer, G. On the construct validity of Rosenzweig's Picture-Frustration Test (PFT). *Proceedings of the XXth International Congress of Psychology, 1972.* Tokyo: Science Council of Japan and University of Tokyo Press, 1974, p. 401 .

Meyer, A.-E., and Weitemeyer, W. Zur Frage der Krankheits-Dependenz des (Phantasierten) Aggressionsverhaltens. *Psyche,* 1967, *21,* 266–282.

Mikawa, J. K., and Boston, J. A. Psychological characteristics of adopted children. *Psychiatric Quarterly Supplement,* 1968, *42,* 274–281.

Mills, D. H. The research use of projective techniques: a seventeen year study. *Journal of Projective Techniques and Personality Assessment,* 1965, *29,* 513–515.

Minski, L., and Desai, M. M. Aspects of personality in peptic ulcer patients; a comparison with hysterics. *British Journal of Medical Psychology,* 1955, *28,* 113–134.

Mintz, M. M. An investigation of the relationship between test anxiety and dependency needs in children. *Dissertation Abstracts,* 1968, *29,* 2206B.

Mirmow, E. L. The method of successive clinical predictions in the validation of projective techniques with special reference to the Rosenzweig Picture-Frustration Study. Unpublished doctoral dissertation, Washington University, (St. Louis), 1952. Summarized in Rosenzweig, 1960, pp. 168–170. (a)

Mirmow, E. L. The Rosenzweig Picture-Frustration Study. In D. Brower and L. E. Abt (Eds.), *Progress in clinical psychology* (Vol. 1). New York: Grune & Stratton, 1952. See Section 1, pp. 209–221. (b)

Misa, K. F. Cognitive, personality, and familial correlates of children's occupational preferences. *Dissertation Abstracts,* 1967, *28,* 1170B.

Misiti, R., and Ponzo, E. Le reazioni alla frustrazione in èta prepuberale nella rappresentazione dell'adulto. *Rivista di Psicologia,* 1958, *52,* 303–309.

Mitchell, K. M. The Rosenzweig Picture-Frustration Study as a measure of reaction to personal evaluation. *Journal of Projective Techniques and Personality Assessment,* 1967, *31,* 65–68.

Miyawaki, J. Hekichi jido no personality no kenkyu: P.F.T. no kekka o chushin to shite [The study of personality traits of rural pupils: primarily based upon the Picture-Frustration Study]. *Japanese Journal of Educational Psychology,* 1958, *6,* 77–84, 132.

Monosoff, H. The comparative effects of rewarding, punishing and counter-conditioning verbal aggressive behavior. *Dissertation Abstracts*, 1964, *24*, 3423.

Moore, M. E., and Schwartz, M. M. The effect of the sex of the frustrated figure on responses to the Rosenzweig P-F Study. *Journal of Projective Techniques*, 1963, *27*, 195–199.

Mordkoff, A. M., and Golas, R. M. Coronary artery disease and response to the Rosenzweig Picture-Frustration Study. *Journal of Abnormal Psychology*, 1968, *73*, 381–386.

Moss, C. S., Jensen, R. E., Morrow, W., and Freund, H. G. Specific behavioral changes produced by chlorpromazine in chronic schizophrenia. *American Journal of Psychiatry*, 1958, *115*, 449–451.

Mouren, P., Dongier, S., and Dongier, D. Evolution des donées du test de Rosenzweig au cours d'une psychotherapie. In *Rapport du congrès des médecins aliénistes et neurologistes de France et des pays de langue française. Bordeaux, 1956*. Paris: Masson, 1957, pp. 318–324.

Mukerji, K., and Debabrata, B. Relationship between the direction of aggression and self-perceived problem-variables among a group of offenders. *Indian Journal of Psychology*, 1968, *43*, 37–40.

Murphy, A. T., Jr. An electroencephalographic study of frustration in stutterers. *Speech Monographs*, 1953, *20*, 148.

Murphy, M. M. Social class differences in frustration patterns of alcoholics. *Quarterly Journal of Studies on Alcohol*, 1956, *17*, 255–262 .

Musgrove, W. J. A study of type of reaction to frustration and direction of aggression in one parent families and in two parent families. *Dissertation Abstracts*, 1965, *26*, 6516.

Myklebust, H. R. The psychosocial adjustment of children with dyslexia. *Dissertation Abstracts*, 1969, *29*, 3456A.

Nathan, P. E. Conceptual ability and indices of frustration tolerance on the Rosenzweig Picture-Frustration Study. *Journal of Projective Techniques*, 1963, *27*, 200–207.

Nava, J., and Cunha, S. Ezequiel da. Agressividade e condução de veiculos: avaliação por meio de teste de aplicacao coletiva (P-F de Rosenzweig), comparado a um teste individual (P.M.K. de Mira). In J. Nava et al, *Aspec-*

tos da personalidade em seleção de condutores de veiculos. Belo Horizonte, Brazil: Editora Itatiaia, 1957, pp. 73–91. (a)

Nava, J., and Cunha, S. Ezequiel da. Aplicação economica do P-F de Rosenzweig em grupos. In J. Nava et al. *Aspectos da personalidade em seleção de condutores de veiculos.* Belo Horizonte, Brazil: Editora Itatiaia, 1957, pp. 45–71. (b)

Němec, J. The motivation background of hyperkinetic dysphonia in children: a contribution to psychologic research in phoniatry. *Logos,* 1961, *4,* 28–31.

Němes, Livia. Külöleges reakciók és választások értelmezése a frusztrácios próbában (PFT) [Interpretation of specific reactions and choices in the Picture-Frustration Test (PFT).]. *Magyar Pszichologiai Szemle,* 1968, *25,* 553–563.

Nencini, R. Contributo alla validazione fattoriale di interpretazioni psicodiag-nostiche. *Contributi dell'Istituto Nazionale Psicologia del Consiglio Nationale Ricerche, Rome,* 1956–1958. *Bollettino di Psicologia Applicata,* 1962, No. 53–54, 3–38.

Nencini, R. Valore delle tecniche proiettive per la comprensione dei dinamismi inconsci e dei loro effetti a livello di comportamento. *Medicina Psicosomatica,* 1959, *4,* 3–19.

Nencini, R. Nuova taratura del P.F.S. di Rosenzweig. *Bollettino di Psicologia Applicata,* 1965, No. 71–72, 3–22.

Nencini, R., and Banissoni, P. Contributo alla taratura italiana del P.F. Test di Rosenzweig. *Archivio di Psicologia, Neurologia e Psichiatria,* 1954, *15,* 313–332.

Nencini, R., Banissoni, P., and Misiti, R. *Taratura italiana del Picture-Frustration Study secondo i criteri originali di S. Rosenzweig* (Supplemento al Manuale). Florence: Organizzazioni Speciali, 1958. (Supplement to the Manual of the Italian version of the Rosenzweig P-F Study, Adult Form)

Nencini, R., and Belcecchi, M. V. *Guida alla forma per adulti del P.F.S. di Rosenzweig.* Florence: Organizzazioni Speciali, 1976. (Current Manual for the Italian version of the Rosenzweig P-F Study, Adult Form)

Nencini, R., and Casini Nencini, M. G. Contributo all'applicazione del P.F.T. di Rosenzweig in campo psichatrico. *Bollettino di Psicologia e Sociologia Applicate,* 1957, No. 19–20, 17–34.

Nencini, R., and Misiti, R. Contributo all'identificazione di "tipi" psicologici sulla base delle reazioni alla frustrazione nel P.F.T. di Rosenzweig. *Bollettino di Psicologia e Sociologia Applicata,* 1956, No. 17–18, 48–74. (a)

Nencini, R., and Misiti, R. Contributo alla validazione del P.F.T. di Rosenzweig. *Rivista di Psicologia,* 1956, *50,* 37–75. (b)

Nencini, R., Misiti, R., and Banissoni, P. Possibilità diagnostiche del P.F. Test di Rosenzweig in psichiatria. *Il Lavoro Neuropsichiatrico,* 1954, *15,* 189–207.

Nencini, R., Reda, G. C., Schiavi, F., and Alliani, E. Il P.F. Test di Rosenzweig in tronta tentativi di suicidio. *Archivio di Psicologia, Neurologia e Psichiatria,* 1953, *14,* 289–306.

Nencini, R., and Riccio, D. Il P.F. Test di Rosenzweig nella psiconevrosi ossessivo-compulsiva. *Bollettino di Psicologia e Sociologia Applicate,* 1957, No. 21–24, 71–84.

Nencini, R., and Venier, N. Comportamento "stereotipato" e scelte "logiche" nelle reazioni alla frustrazioni. *Bollettino di Psicologia Applicata,* 1966, No. 77–78, 3–19. (a)

Nencini, R., and Venier, N. Influenza delle caratteristiche dello stimolo sulle reazioni alla frustrazione. *Bollettino di Psicologia Applicata,* 1966, No. 73–76, 45–55. (b)

Nick, E. *Teste de Frustração. Manual, Forma para Adultos.* Rio de Janeiro: Centro Editor de Psicologia Aplicada, 1970. (Manual for the Portuguese version of the Rosenzweig P-F Study, Adult Form)

Nisenson, R. A. Aggressive reactions to frustration in relation to the individual level of extrapunitiveness. *Journal of Personality Assessment,* 1972, *36,* 50–54.

Norman, R. D., and Kleinfeld, G. R. Rosenzweig Picture-Frustration Study results with minority group juvenile delinquents. *Journal of Genetic Psychology,* 1958, *92,* 61–67.

O'Connell, W. E. Creativity in humor. *Journal of Social Psychology,* 1969, *78,* 237–241.

Oeser, O. A., and Emery, F. E. The emergent personality. Chapter XIII In O. A. Oeser and F. E. Emery (Eds.), *Social structure and personality in a rural community.* Studies of social behavior, New York: Macmillan, 1954, pp. 201–203, 242.

Osis, K., and Fahler, J. Space and time variables in ESP. *Journal of the American Society for Psychical Research,* 1965, *59,* 130–145.

Otsu, K. The misrecognition of situations in the Picture-Frustration Study for Children. *Psychological Test Bulletin* (Kyoto City, Japan: Sankyobo) 1961, *1,* 16–21.

Palmer, J. O. Some relationships between Rorschach's experience balance and Rosenzweig's frustration-aggression patterns. *Journal of Projective Techniques,* 1957, *21,* 137–141.

Pareek, U. Reliability of the Indian adaptation of the Rosenzweig P-F Study (Children's Form). *Journal of Psychological Researches* (Madras, India), 1958, *2,* 18–23. (a)

Pareek, U. Some preliminary data about the Indian adaptation of the Rosenzweig P-F Study (Children's Form). *Education and Psychology* (Delhi), 1958, *5,* 105–113. (b)

Pareek, U. Studying cultural differences in personality development with the help of the Rosenzweig P-F study. *Pratibha (Journal of the All-India Institute of Mental Health* Bangalore, India), 1958, *1,* 115–123. (c)

Pareek, U. Validity of the Indian adaptation of the Rosenzweig P-F Study (Children's Form), *Psychological Newsletter* (New York University), 1958, *10,* 28–40. (d)

Pareek, U. Rosenzweig Picture-Frustration Study—a review. *Psychological Newsletter* (New York University), 1959, *10,* 98–114. (a)

Pareek, U. Scoring samples of Indian children on the Rosenzweig P-F Study. *Naya Shikshak* (Bikaner, India), April, 1959. (b)

Pareek, U. *Children's reactions to frustration* (C.I.E. Publication No. 44). Delhi: Central Institute of Education, 1960. (a)

Pareek, U. Developmental patterns of Rosenzweig P-F Study variables in Indian children. *Manas* (Delhi), 1960, *7,* 19–35. (b)

Pareek, U. An investigation of the validity of the Indian adaptation of the Rosenzweig Picture-Frustration Study (Children's Form). *Indian Journal of Psychology,* 1960, *35,* 71–88. (c)

Pareek, U. *Developmental patterns in reactions to frustration.* New York: Asia Publishing House, 1964.

Pareek, U., and Devi, R. S. Reliability of the Adult Form of the Indian adaptation of the Rosenzweig P-F Study. *Indian Journal of Psychology,* 1965, *40,* 67–71.

Pareek, U., Devi, R. S., and Rosenzweig, S. *Manual of the Indian adaptation of the Rosenzweig Picture-Frustration Study, Adult Form.* Varanasi, India: Rupa Psychological Corp., 1968.

Pareek, U., and Kumar, V. K. Establishing criteria for significance of trends for the adult form of the Rosenzweig P-F Study. *Research Bulletin of the Department of Psychology, Osmania University,* 1966, *2,* 29–35.

Pareek, U., and Rosenzweig, S. *Manual of the Indian adaptation of the Rosenzweig Picture-Frustration Study, Children's Form.* Delhi: Mânasâyan, 1959.

Parsons, E. T. Relationship between the Rosenzweig P-F Study and test duration, socioeconomic status, and religion. *Journal of Consulting Psychology,* 1955, *19,* 28.

Pasquet, P., Laboureur, P., and Caille, E. J. P. Résultate d'examen psychologique. Analyse concernant 100 malades d'un service ouvert de psychiatrie par le méthode des tests. *Annales Médico-Psychologiques,* 1955, *113,* 548–557.

Pavlovic, L. An attempt to use the Rosenzweig Picture-Frustration Study as a social intelligence test. *Resumés, XVᵉ Congress International de Psychologie Appliquée* (Ljubljana, August 1964). Belgrade, 1964.

Peizer, S. B. Effect of incarceration on the direction of aggressive behavior. *Journal of Correctional Psychology,* 1956, *1,* 1–2; 26–31.

Perczel, J., and Perczel, T. Description and measurement of personality traits by a projective technique and an auto-definition questionnaire with production engineering inspectors. *British Journal of Projective Psychology and Personality Study,* 1969, *14,* 27–29.

Petiziol, A., and Ricco, D. Il PFT di Rosenzweig in un gruppo di donne dedite alla prostituzione abituale. *Schweizerische Zeitschrift für Psychologie und ihre Anwendungen,* Beiheft Nr. 40, 1960, 176–180.

Petrauskas, F. B. A TAT and Picture-Frustration study of naval offenders and non-offenders. Ph.D. dissertation, Loyola University (Chicago), 1958. Summarized in Chapter 11 of *Story Sequence Analysis* by Magda Arnold. New York: Columbia University Press, 1962.

Pflanz, M., and von Uexkull;, T. Psychosomatische Untersuchungen an Hoch-druckkranken. *Medizinische Klinik,* 1962, *57,* 345–351.

Picard, P., Grousset, C., and Pasquet, P. Le P.F. Test en pathologie mentale. *Rapport du congrès des médecine aliénistes et neurologistes de France et des pays de langue française. Bordeaux, 1956.* Paris: Masson, 1957, pp. 274–285.

Pichot, P. L'évolution de L'emploi et des, recherches sur les tests mentaux aux Etats-Unis. *Revue de Psychologie Appliquée,* 1954, *4,* 317–340.

Pichot, P. La validité des techniques projectives: problèmes généraux. *Revue de Psychologie Appliquée,* 1955, *5,* 235–244.

Pichot, P., and Cardinet, J. Les profils, les patterns et les tendances dans le Test de Frustration de Rosenzweig. Standardisation et etalonnage français. *Revue de Psychologie Appliquée,* 1955, *5,* 127–142.

Pichot, P., and Danjon, S. Le test de frustration de Rosenzweig. *Revue de Psychologie Appliquée,* 1951, *1,* 147–225. (Manual for the French version of the Rosenzweig P-F Study, Adult Form)

Pichot, P., and Danjon, S. La fidélite du Test de Frustration de Rosenzweig. *Revue de Psychologie Appliquée,* 1955, *5,* 1–11.

Pichot, P., and Danjon, S., Manuel du test de frustration de Rosenzweig. Paris: Centre de Psychologie Appliquée, 1956. (New and enlarged edition of the Manual for the French version of the Rosenzweig P-F Study, Adult Form)

Pichot, P., Freson, V., and Danjon, S. *Le test de frustration de Rosenzweig: forme pour enfants. Revue de Psychologie Appliquée,* 1956, *6,* 111–138. (Manual for the French version of the Rosenzweig P-F Study, Children Form)

Pierloot, R. A., and Van Roy, J. Asthma and aggression. *Journal of Psychosomatic Research,* 1969, *13,* 333–337.

Pitkänen, L. The effect of spaced vs. massed presentation of aggression items on verbal aggressive responses of children. *Scandinavian Journal of Psychology,* 1963, *4,* 55–64.

Pitkänen, L. *A descriptive model of aggression and nonaggression with applications to children's behaviour. Jyväskylä Studies in Education, Psychology and Social Research,* No. 19. Jyväskylä, Finland: Jyväskylän Yliopiston kirjasto, 1969.

Popp, M. Eine empirische Untersuchung über die Stabilität der Aggressions-richtung. *Psychologie in Erziehung und Unterricht.,* 1974, *21,* 91–99.

Portnoy, B., and Stacey, C. L. A comparative study of Negro and white subnor-mals on the children's form of the Rosenzweig P-F Test. *American Journal of Mental Deficiency,* 1954, *59,* 272–278.

Prensky, S. J. An investigation of some personality characteristics of epileptic and psychosomatic patients: an evaluation of certain personality measures and reactions to frustration in idiopathic epileptic, symptomatic epileptic, and peptic ulcer patients. *Dissertation Abstracts,* 1958–59, *19,* 3025.

Preston, C. E. Accident-proneness in attempted suicide and in automobile acci-dent victims. *Journal of Consulting Psychology,* 1964, *28,* 79–82.

Purdom, G. A., Jr. Comparison of performance of competent and incompetent readers in a state training school for delinquent boys on the WAIS and the Rosenzweig P-F Study. *Dissertation Abstracts,* 1958–59, *19,* 1016–1017.

Pym, D. A study of frustration and aggression among factory and office workers. *Occupational Psychology,* 1963, *37,* 165–179.

Pym, D. Exploring characteristics of the versatile worker. *Occupational Psy-chology,* 1965, *39,* 271–278.

Quarrington, B. The performance of stutterers on the Rosenzweig Picture-Frustration test. *Journal of Clinical Psychology,* 1953, *9,* 189–192.

Quay, H., and Sweetland, A. The relationship of the Rosenzweig Picture-Frus-tration Study to the M.M.P.I. *Journal of Clinical Psychology,* 1954, *10,* 296–297.

Rao, T. V., and Ramalingaswamy, P. A study of reactions to frustration and intelligence levels of fifth-grade children of Delhi schools. *Indian Educa-tional Review,* 1974, *9,* 38–47.

Rapaport, G. M., and Marshall, R. J. The prediction of rehabilitative potential of stockade prisoners using clinical psychological tests. *Journal of Clinical Psychology,* 1962, *18,* 444–446.

Rapisarda, V. Il test di frustrazione di Rosenzweig nei nevrotici. *Igiene Men-tale,* 1960, *4,* 3–7.

Rapisarda, V. *Validità e taratura regionale del Picture Frustration Study.* Catania: Quaderni di "Orpheus," 1962.

Rapisarda, V., and Mastruzzo, A. Reazioni alla frustrazione in un gruppo di giovani ciclisti. *Igiene Mentale,* 1960, *4,* 675–688. (a)

Rapisarda, V., and Mastruzzo, A. Indagine sulla tolleranza alle frustrazioni in un gruppo di soggetti praticanti sollevamento pesi. *Igiene Mentale,* 1960, *4,* 721–729. (b)

Rapisarda, V., and Romeo, G. Lo studio della frustrazione degli ulcerosi. *Revista di Psicologia,* 1965, *59,* 444–450.

Rauchfleisch, U. Neue Interpretationsmöglichkeiten des Rosenzweig-Picture-Frustration-Tests durch Verwendung von Indizes. *Schweizerische Zeitschrift für Psychologie und ihre Anwendungen,* 1971, *30,* 299–311. (a)

Rauchfleisch, U. Der Rosenzweig P-F Test in der klinisch-psychodiagnostischen Praxis: Eine Untersuchung an psychisch Gesunden, Süchtigen und Neurotikern. *Zeitschrift für Psychotherapie und medizinische Psychologie,* 1971, *21,* 151–159. (b)

Rauchfleisch, U. Frustrationsreaktionen verwahrloster Jugendlicher im Rosenzweig Picture-Frustration-Test. *Zeitschrift für klinische Psychologie und Psychotherapie,* 1973, *21,* 18–25.

Rauchfleisch, U. Beziehungen zwischen Frustrationsreaktionen und Intelligenzfunktionen bei verwahrlosten Jugendlichen. *Psychologische Beiträge,* 1974, *16,* 365–397.

Rauchfleisch, U. Zur Frage der diagnostischen Bedeutung der "Diskrepanzen" im Progressiven Matrizentest von Raven. *Diagnostica: Zeitschrift für psychologische Diagnostik,* 1975, *21,* 107–115.

Rauchfleisch, U. Frustrationsverhalten und intellektuelle Anpassungsfunktionen bei verwahrlosten Kindern und Jugendlichen. *Heilpädagogische Forschung,* 1976, *6,* 308–316.

Rauchfleisch, U. *Handbuch zum Rosenzweig Picture-Frustration Test (PFT). Grundlagen, bisherige Resultate und Andwendungsmöglichkeiten des PFT* (Vol. 1). *Handanweisung zur Durchführung des PFT und Neueichung der Testformen für Kinder und Erwachsene* (Vol. 2). Bern: Huber, 1978.

Reck, J. J., McCary, J. L., and Weatherly, J. K. Intra-familial comparisons of frustration-aggression patterns. *Psychological Reports*, 1969, *25*, 356.

Reid, L. L. An evaluation of the Rosenzweig Picture-Frustration Test. *West Virginia University Bulletin*, 1951, *23*, 170–172.

Reynolds, A. E. Evaluation of an institutional attendant training project. *Dissertation Abstracts*, 1972, *32*, 4195B.

Riccio, D., and Antonelli, F. Il "P.F.T. di Rosenzweig" in 21 pugili italiani partecipanti alle olimpiadi di Roma. *Archivo di Psicologia, Neurologia e Psichiatria*, 1962, *23*, 329–346.

Ricciuti, E. A. Children and radio: a study of listeners and non-listeners to various types of radio programs in terms of selected ability, attitude, and behavior measures. *Genetic Psychology Monographs*, 1951, *44*, 69–143.

Roberts, A. H., and Jessor, R. Authoritarianism, punitiveness, and perceived social status. *Journal of Abnormal and Social Psychology*, 1958, *56*, 311–314.

Rogers, A. H., and Paul, C. Impunitiveness and unwitting self-evaluation. *Journal of Projective Techniques*, 1959, *23*, 459–461.

Rosenzweig, S. Preferences in the repetition of successful and unsuccessful activities as a function of age and personality. *Journal of Genetic Psychology*, 1933, *42*, 423–441. (a)

Rosenzweig, S. The recall of finished and unfinished tasks as affected by the purpose with which they were performed. *Psychological Bulletin*, 1933, *30*, 698. (Abstract) (b)

Rosenzweig, S. A suggestion for making verbal personality tests more valid. *Psychological Review*, 1934, *41*, 400–401. (a)

Rosenzweig, S. Types of reaction to frustration: a heuristic classification. *Journal of Abnormal and Social Psychology*, 1934, *29*, 298–300. (b)

Rosenzweig, S. A test for types of reaction to frustration. *American Journal of Orthopsychiatry*, 1935, *5*, 395–403.

Rosenzweig, S. The experimental study of psychoanalytic concepts. *Character and Personality*, 1937, *6*, 61–71. (a)

Rosenzweig, S. Frustration as a co-ordinating concept in experimental psychopathology. *Report of National Research Council Conference on Experimental Neuroses and Allied Problems*, 1937, 38–42. (b)

Rosenzweig, S. A dynamic interpretation of psychotherapy oriented towards research. *Psychiatry*, 1938, *1*, 521–526. (a)

Rosenzweig, S. The experimental measurement of types of reaction to frustration. In H. A. Murray (Ed.), *Explorations in personality.* New York: Oxford University Press, 1938, pp. 585–599. (b)

Rosenzweig, S. The experimental study of repression. In H. A. Murray (Ed.), *Explorations in personality.* New York: Oxford University Press, 1938, pp. 472–490. (c)

Rosenzweig, S. Need-persistive and ego-defensive reactions to frustration as demonstrated by an experiment on repression. *Psychological Review*, 1941, *48*, 347–349.

Rosenzweig, S. An experimental study of 'repression' with special reference to need-persistive and ego-defensive reactions to frustration. *Journal of Experimental Psychology*, 1943, *32*, 64–74.

Rosenzweig, S. An outline of frustration theory. Chapter 11 In J. McV. Hunt (Ed.), *Personality and the behavior disorders* (Vol. 1). New York: Ronald Press, 1944.

Rosenzweig, S. The picture-association method and its application in a study of reactions to frustration. *Journal of Personality*, 1945, *14*, 3–23.

Rosenzweig, S. Frustration tolerance and the Picture-Frustration Study. *Psychological Service Center Journal*, 1950, *2*, 109–115. (a)

Rosenzweig, S. Levels of behavior in psychodiagnosis with special reference to the Picture-Frustration Study. *American Journal of Orthopsychiatry*, 1950, *20*, 63–72. (b)

Rosenzweig, S. A method of validation by successive clinical predictions. *Journal of Abnormal and Social Psychology*, 1950, *45*, 507–509. (c)

Rosenzweig, S. Revised norms for the Adult Form of the Rosenzweig Picture-Frustration Study. *Journal of Personality*, 1950, *18*, 344–346. (d)

Rosenzweig, S. Some problems relating to research on the Rosenzweig Picture-Frustration Study. *Journal of Personality*, 1950, *18*, 303–305. (e)

Rosenzweig, S. The treatment of humorous responses in the Rosenzweig Picture-Frustration Study: a note on the revised (1950) instructions. *Journal of Psychology*, 1950, *30*, 139–143. (f)

Rosenzweig, S. *Revised scoring manual for the Rosenzweig Picture-Frustration Study, Form for Adults.* St. Louis: S. Rosenzweig, 1950. (g)

Rosenzweig, S. Idiodynamics in personality theory with special reference to projective methods. *Psychological Review*, 1951, *58*, 213–223. (a)

Rosenzweig, S. The influence of differing methods of administration upon responses to the P-F. Unpublished laboratory report, 1951. (b)

Rosenzweig, S. Laboratory report on miscellaneous P-F Study projects. Unpublished manuscript, 1952.

Rosenzweig, S. Rosenzweig Picture-Frustration Study. Chapter 25B In A. Weider (Ed.), *Contributions toward medical psychology* (Vol. 2). New York: Ronald Press, 1953.

Rosenzweig, S. Projective methods and psychometric criteria: a note of reply to J. P. Sutcliffe. *Australian Journal of Psychology*, 1956, *8*, 152–155. (a)

Rosenzweig, S. Vintage Binet contemporized. *Contemporary Psychology*, 1956, *1*, 219–220. (b)

Rosenzweig, S. The place of the individual and of idiodynamics in psychology: a dialogue. *Journal of Individual Psychology*, 1958, *14*, 3–20.

Rosenzweig, S. The validity of validity. Unpublished manuscript, 1959.

Rosenzweig, S. The Rosenzweig Picture-Frustration Study, Children's Form. In A. I. Rabin and M. Haworth (Eds.), *Projective techniques with children.* New York: Grune & Stratton, 1960, pp. 149–176.

Rosenzweig, S. Le Test de Frustration de Rosenzweig pour enfants: développment et état actuel. *Revue de Psychologie Appliquée*, 1962, *12*, 275–310.

Rosenzweig, S. Validity of the Rosenzweig Picture-Frustration Study with felons and delinquents. *Journal of Consulting Psychology*, 1963, *27*, 535–536.

Rosenzweig, S. Il Picture Frustration Study forma per fanciulli. *Bolletino di Psicologia Applicata*, 1964, No. 61–62, 1–31.

Rosenzweig, S. Note of correction for Schwartz, Cohen and Pavlik's "The effects of subject- and experimenter-induced defensive response sets on Picture-Frustration Test reactions." *Journal of Projective Techniques and Personality Assessment,* 1965, *29,* 352–353.

Rosenzweig, S. Extending the repressor-sensitizer dichotomy. *Journal of Clinical Psychology,* 1967, *23,* 37–38. (a)

Rosenzweig, S. Revised criteria for the Group Conformity Rating of the Rosenzweig Picture-Frustration Study, Adult Form. *Journal of Projective Techniques and Personality Assessment,* 1967, *31,* 58–61. (b)

Rosenzweig, S. A brief semicentennial survey of child guidance practices (1909–1959). *Journal of Genetic Psychology,* 1968, *112,* 109–116.

Rosenzweig, S. Différences de réactions a la frustration entre adolescents et adolescentes. *Revue de Psychologie Appliquée.* 1969, *19,* 91–104.

Rosenzweig, S. Sex différences in réaction to frustration among adolescents. In J. Zubin and A. Freedman (Eds.), *Psychopathology of adolescence.* New York: Grune & Stratton, 1970, pp. 90–107. (a)

Rosenzweig, S. A comparative investigation of P-F Study results under multiple-choice and standard procedures of administration. Unpublished investigation, 1970. (b)

Rosenzweig, S. Aggressive behavior and the Rosenzweig Picture-Frustration (P-F) Study. *Journal of Clinical Psychology,* 1976, *32,* 885–891. (a)

Rosenzweig, S. L'aggression et le Test de Frustration de Rosenzweig. *Revue de Psychologie Appliquée,* 1976, *26,* 39–48. (b)

Rosenzweig, S. Manual for the Rosenzweig Picture-Frustration Study, Adolescent Form. St. Louis: S. Rosenzweig, 1976. (c)

Rosenzweig, S. *Manual for the Children's Form of the Rosenzweig Picture-Frustration (P-F) Study.* St. Louis: Rana House, 1977. (a)

Rosenzweig, S. Outline of a denotative definition of aggression. *Aggressive Behavior,* 1977, *3,* 379–383. (b)

Rosenzweig, S. Rosenzweig Picture-Frustration (P-F) Study. In B. B. Wolman (Ed.), *International encyclopedia of psychiatry, psychology, psychoanalysis and neurology,* 1977, *9,* 483–486. (c)

Rosenzweig, S. *The Rosenzweig Picture-Frustration (P-F) Study: Basic Manual.* St. Louis: Rana House, 1978. (a)

Rosenzweig, S. *Adult Form Supplement to the Basic Manual of the Rosenzweig Picture-Frustration (P-F) Study.* St. Louis: Rana House, 1978. (b)

Rosenzweig, S., and Adelman, S. Construct validity of the Rosenzweig Picture-Frustration Study. *Journal of Personality Assessment,* 1977, *41,* 578–588.

Rosenzweig, S., and Braun, S. H. Differenze dipendenti dal sasso nelle reazioni degli adolescenti nella frustrazione. Esaminate con il P. F. Study di Rosenzweig. *Bollettino di Psicologia Applicata,* 1969, No. 91–93, 23–33.

Rosenzweig, S., and Braun, S. H. Adolescent sex differences in reactions to frustration as explored by the Rosenzweig P-F Study. *Journal of Genetic Psychology,* 1970, *116,* 53–61.

Rosenzweig, S., Bundas, L. E., Lumry, K., and Davidson, H. W. An elementary syllabus of psychological tests. *Journal of Psychology,* 1944, *18,* 9–40. See pp. 28–29.

Rosenzweig, S., Clarke, H. J., Garfield, M. S., and Lehndorff, A. Scoring samples for the Rosenzweig Picture-Frustration Study. *Journal of Psychology,* 1946, *21,* 45–72.

Rosenzweig, S., Fleming, E. E., and Clarke, H. J. Revised scoring manual for the Rosenzweig Picture-Frustration Study. *Journal of Psychology,* 1947, *24,* 165–208.

Rosenzweig, S., Fleming, E. E., and Rosenzweig, L. The Children's Form of the Rosenzweig Picture-Frustration Study. *Journal of Psychology,* 1948, *26,* 141–191.

Rosenzweig, S., with Kogan, K. Rosenzweig Picture-Frustration Study. In *Psychodiagnosis: an introduction to the integration of tests in dynamic clinical practice.* New York: Grune & Stratton, 1949, pp. 167–182.

Rosenzweig, S., Ludwig, D. J., and Adelman, S. Esame della fedeltà mediante la tecnica del retest del Rosenzweig Picture Frustration Study e di techniche semi-proiettive simili. *Bollettino di Psicologia Applicata,* 1973, No. 118–120, 5–18.

Rosenzweig, S., Ludwig, D. J., and Adelman, S. Fidélite test-retest du Test de Frustration de Rosenzweig et de techniques semi-projectives analogues. *Revue de Psychologie Appliquée,* 1974, *24,* 181–196.

Rosenzweig, S., Ludwig, D. J., and Adelman, S. Retest reliability of the Rosenzweig Picture-Frustration Study and similar semi-projective techniques. *Journal of Personality Assessment*, 1975, *39*, 3–12.

Rosenzweig, S., and Mason, G. A. An experimental study of memory in relation to the theory of repression. *British Journal of Psychology*, 1934, *24*, 247–265.

Rosenzweig, S., and Mirmow, E. L. The validation of trends in the Children's Form of the Rosenzweig Picture-Frustration Study. *Journal of Personality*, 1950, *18*, 306–314.

Rosenzweig, S., Mowrer, O. H., Haslerud, G. M., Curtis, Q. F., and Barker, R. G. Frustration as an experimental problem. *Character and Personality*, 1938, *7*, 126–160.

Rosenzweig, S., and Rosenzweig, L. Aggression in problem children and normals as evaluated by the Rosenzweig P-F Study. *Journal of Abnormal and Social Psychology*, 1952, *47*, 683–687.

Rosenzweig, S., and Rosenzweig, L. *Guide to research on the Rosenzweig Picture-Frustration (P-F) Study, 1934–1974, organized by topic; and Bibliography of research: References by author.* St. Louis: S. and L. Rosenzweig, 1975.

Rosenzweig, S., and Rosenzweig, L. Guide to research on the Rosenzweig Picture-Frustration (P-F) Study, 1934–1974. *Journal of Personality Assessment*, 1976, *40*, 599–606. (a)

Rosenzweig, S., and Rosenzweig, L. Guida alla ricerca sul Rosenzweig Picture-Frustration (P-F) Study, 1934–1974. *Bollettino di Psicologia Applicata*, 1976, No. 133–134–135, 3–15. (b)

Rosenzweig, S., and Rosenzweig, L. Guide pour la recherche sur le Test de Frustration de Rosenzweig, 1934–1974. *Revue de Psychologie Appliquée*, 1977, *27*, 51–61.

Rosenzweig, S., and Sarason, S. An experimental study of the triadic hypothesis: reaction to frustration, ego-defense, and hypnotizability: I. Correlational approach. *Character and Personality*, 1942, *11*, 1–19.

Ross, E. N. Reactions to frustration of retardates in special and in regular classes. *Dissertation Abstracts*, 1965, *26*, 2316.

Ross, W. D., Adsett, N., Gleser, G., Joyce, C. R. B., Kaplan, S. M., and Tieger,

M. E. A trial of psychopharmacologic measurement with projective techniques. *Journal of Projective Techniques and Personality Assessment,* 1963, *27,* 222–225.

Roth, R. M. & Puri, P. Direction of aggression and the non-achievement syndrome. *Journal of Counseling Psychology,* 1967, *14,* 277–281.

Sacco, F. Studio della frustrazione col P-F di Rosenzweig nei siciliani in eta evolutiva. *Infanzia anormale,* 1955, *11,* 146–166.

Sacripanti, P. Il P.F.T. di Rosenzweig negli stati depressivi. *Neuropsichiatria,* 1958, *1,* 93.

Saito, I. Social status, out-or-in-group, and aggressive behavior in Japanese society. *Japanese Journal of Psychology,* 1973, *44,* 150–155.

Saltzman, E. S. A comparison of patterns of identification as shown by family members of three religious denominations in Houston, Texas. *Dissertation Abstracts,* 1965, *26,* 6857.

Sanford, F. H. The use of a projective device in attitude surveying. *Public Opinion Quarterly,* 1950–51, *14,* 697–709.

Sanford, F. H., and Rosenstock, I. M. Projective techniques on the doorstep. *Journal of Abnormal and Social Psychology,* 1952, *47,* 3–16.

Sarason, S., and Rosenzweig, S. An experimental study of the triadic hypothesis: reaction to frustration, ego-defense, and hypnotizability: II. Thematic apperception approach. *Character and Personality,* 1942, *11,* 150–165.

Sarker, S. N. Reactions of the tribal Hindu and tribal Christian girls to common stress-producing situations. *Indian Psychological Review,* 1969, *5,* 146–149.

Sarnoff, I. Identification with the aggressor: some personality correlates of anti-Semitism among Jews. *Journal of Personality,* 1951, *20,* 199–218.

Schalock, R. L., and MacDonald, P. Personality variables associated with reactions to frustration. *Journal of Projective Techniques and Personality Assessment,* 1966, *30,* 158–160.

Schill, T. R., and Black, J. M. Differences in reaction to frustration as a function of need for approval. *Psychological Reports,* 1967, *21,* 87–88.

Schill, T., and Black, J. M. Differences in reactions to Rosenzweig's P-F Study by defensive and nondefensive repressors and sensitizers. *Psychological Reports*, 1969, *25*, 929–930.

Schmeidler, G. R. Some relations between Picture-Frustration ratings and ESP scores. *Journal of Personality*, 1950, *18*, 331–343.

Schmeidler, G. R. Picture-Frustration ratings and ESP scores for subjects who showed moderate annoyance at the ESP task. *Journal of Parapsychology*, 1954, *18*, 137–152.

Schmeidler, G. R., and McConnell, R. A. Frustration in relation to ESP. In *ESP and personality patterns*. New Haven: Yale University Press, 1958.

Schneider, J. E. The effects of a season of competition on the aggressive responses of intercollegiate football players. *Dissertation Abstracts*, 1974, *34*, 6434A.

Schöfer, G., and Meyer, A.-E. Krankheitsbedingte Veränderungen bei den Reaktionen im Rosenzweig Picture Frustration Test (PFT). *Medizinische Psychologie*, 1976, *2*, 1–12.

Schwartz, A. N., and Kleemeier, R. W. The effects of illness and age upon some aspects of personality. *Journal of Gerontology*, 1965, *20*, 85–91.

Schwartz, M. M. The relationship between projective test scoring categories and activity preferences. *Genetic Psychology Monographs*, 1952, *46*, 133–181.

Schwartz, M. M. Galvanic skin responses accompanying the Picture-Frustration Study. *Journal of Clinical Psychology*, 1957, *13*, 382–387. (a)

Schwartz, M. M. The importance of the pictorial aspect in determining performance on the Picture-Frustration Study. *Journal of Clinical Psychology*, 1957, *13*, 399–402. (b)

Schwartz, M. M., Cohen, B. D., and Pavlik, W. B. Effects of subject-and-experimenter-induced defensive response sets on picture-frustration test reactions. *Journal of Projective Techniques and Personality Assessment*, 1964, *28*, 341–345.

Schwartz, M. M., and Karlin, L. A new technique for studying the meaning of performance on the Rosenzweig Picture-Frustration Study. *Journal of Consulting Psychology*, 1954, *18*, 131–134.

Schwartz, M. M., and Levine, H. Union and management leaders: a comparison. *Personnel Administration,* 1965, *28,* 44–47.

Scott, M. V. Death, anxiety, and attitudes toward violence and aggression. *Dissertation Abstracts,* 1976, *37,* 989B.

Searle, A. The perception of filmed violence by aggressive individuals with high or low self-concept of aggression. *European Journal of Social Psychology,* 1976, *6,* 175–190.

Sears, P. S., and Sherman, V. S. *In pursuit of self-esteem. Case studies of eight elementary school children.* Belmont, Calif.: Wadsworth Publishing Co., 1964.

Seidman, E. Some relationships of frustration reaction to aspects of conscience and social reality. *Dissertation Abstracts,* 1964, *26,* 2316.

Seitz, P. F. D., Gosman, J. S., and Craton, A. B. Super-ego aggression in circumscribed neurodermatitis. *Journal of Investigative Dermatology,* 1953, *20,* 263–269.

Selkin, J., and Morris, J. Some behavioral factors which influence the recovery rate of suicide attempters. *Bulletin of Suicidology,* 1971, *8,* 29–38.

Semeonoff, B. *Projective techniques.* New York: John Wiley, 1976. See pp. 156–160.

Seward, G. H., Morrison, L. M., and Fost, B. Personality structure in a common form of colitis. *Psychological Monographs,* 1951, *65* (Whole No. 318).

Shakow, D., Rodnick, E. H., and Lebeaux, T. A psychological study of a schizophrenic: exemplification of a method. *Journal of Abnormal and Social Psychology,* 1945, *40,* 154–174.

Shapiro, A. E. A comparative evaluation of the reactions to frustration of delinquent and non-delinquent male adolescents. *Dissertation Abstracts,* 1954, *14,* 400–401.

Sharma, C. M. Sex differences among adolescents related to reactions to frustration in school situations. *Rajasthan Board Journal of Education* (Rajasthan, India), 1975, *11,* 6–11.

Shaw, M. C., and Black, M. D. The reaction to frustration of bright high school underachievers. *California Journal of Educational Research*, 1960, *11*, 120–124.

Sheehan, J. G. Projective studies of stuttering. *Journal of Speech and Hearing Disorders*, 1958, *23*, 18–25.

Shimazu, M. Comment on the P-F Study. *Psychological Test Bulletin*, (Kyoto City, Japan: Sankyobo), 1961, *1*, 34–36.

Shor, R. E., Orne, M. T., and O'Connell, D. N. Psychological correlates of plateau hypnotizability in a special volunteer sample. *Journal of Personality and Social Psychology*, 1966, *3*, 80–95.

Siegel, S., Spilka, B., and Miller, L. The direction of manifest hostility: its measurement and meaning. *American Psychologist*, 1957, *12*, 421. (Abstract)

Silverstein, A. B. Faking on the Rosenzweig P-F Study. *Journal of Applied Psychology*, 1957, *41*, 192–194.

Simkins, L. Generalization effects of hostile verb reinforcement as a function of stimulus similarity and type of reinforcer. *Journal of Personality*, 1961, *29*, 64–72.

Simons, H. Über die Auswirkungen unterschiedlicher instruktions-bedingungen im Rosenzweig Picture-Frustration Test auf die Antworten von Schülern. *Archiv für die gesamte Psychologie*, 1967, *119*, 16–25. (a)

Simons, H. Zur gruppenspezifischen Diskriminationsfähigkeit der Kinderform des Rosenzweig Picture-Frustration Test. *Diagnostica: Zeitschrift für psychologische Diagnostik*, 1967, *13*, 15–29. (b)

Simos, I. The Picture-Frustration Study in the psychiatric situation—preliminary findings. *Journal of Personality*, 1950, *18*, 327–330.

Sinaiko, M. W. The Rosenzweig Picture-Frustration Study in the selection of department store section managers. *Journal of Applied Psychology*, 1949, *33*, 36–42.

Singh, M. V., Paliwal, T. R., and Gupta, S. Frustration reaction among emotionally disturbed children. *Child Psychiatry Quarterly* (Hyderabad, India), 1972, *5*, 3–10.

Sivanandam, C. A study of frustration-reaction in delinquent and non-delinquent children. *Indian Journal of Social Work*, 1971, *32*, 151–154.

Smith, L. M. The concurrent validity of six personality and adjustment tests for children. *Psychological Monographs,* 1958, *72* (Whole No. 457).

Smith, S. K., Jr. A factor analytic study of the Rosenzweig Picture-Frustration Study as a predictor of academic achievement. *Dissertation Abstracts,* 1961, *22,* 647–648.

Snyders, G. Quel type de frustration atteint le Test de Rosenzweig. *Psychologie Française,* 1961, *6,* 148–152.

Solomon, L. G. An investigation of visual defect and certain cultural and personality factors in juvenile delinquency. *Dissertation Abstracts,* 1962, *25,* 2617.

Sommer, R. On the Brown adaptation of the Rosenzweig P-F for assessing social attitudes. *Journal of Abnormal and Social Psychology,* 1954, *49,* 125–128.

Sopchak, A. L. Projective study of Peter and his parents. *Journal of Child Psychiatry,* 1956, *3,* 149–200.

Spache, G. Differential scoring of the Rosenzweig Picture-Frustration Study. *Journal of Clinical Psychology,* 1950, *6,* 406–408.

Spache, G. Sex differences in the Rosenzweig P-F Study, Children's Form. *Journal of Clinical Psychology,* 1951, *7,* 235–238.

Spache, G. D. Personality characteristics of retarded readers as measured by the Picture-Frustration Study. *Educational and Psychological Measurement,* 1954, *14,* 186–192.

Spache, G. D. Appraising the personality of remedial pupils. In *Education in a free world.* Washington, D.C.: American Council on Education, 1955, pp. 122–131.

Spache, G. D. Personality patterns of retarded readers. *Journal of Educational Research,* 1957, *50,* 461–469.

Spache, G. D. *Toward better reading.* Champaign, Ill.: Garrard Publishing Co., 1963. See pp. 120–121, 130, 439.

Starer, E. Aggressive reactions and sources of frustration in anxiety neurotics and paranoid schizophrenics. *Journal of Clinical Psychology,* 1952, *8,* 307–309.

Stern, E. Neuere experimentelle Methoden zur Untersuchung der Affektivität und des Characters. *Fortschritte der Neurologie, Psychiatrie und ihrer Grenzgebiete,* 1952, *20,* 209–236.

Stern, E. Le test de Rosenzweig en neuro-psychiatrie infantile. *Psyché* (Paris), 1954, *87,* 35–46.

Stern, E. *Die Tests in der klinischen Psychologie* (2 vols.) Zürich: Rascher Verlag, 1954–55. See pages 650-655 in Vol. I.

Stoltz, R. E., and Smith, M. D. Some effects of socio-economic, age and sex factors on children's responses to the Rosenzweig Picture-Frustration Study. *Journal of Clinical Psychology,* 1959, *15,* 200–203.

Sumita, K. Factor analytic investigation of the P-F Study. *Psychological Test Bulletin* (Kyoto City, Japan: Sankyobo), 1961, *1,* 1–6.

Sumita, K., Hayashi, K., and Ichitani, T. *Rosenzweig's personality theory.* Kyoto City: Sankyobo, 1964. (English abstract: *Psychological Abstracts,* 1965, *39,* 1445.)

Sundgren, P. Lärarpersonlighet: Några personlighetsdifferenser mellan olika kategorier sökande till klasslärarutbildning. *Pedagogisk-psykologiska problem* (Malmö, Sweden: Lärarhögskolan), 1964, No. 4. (a)

Sundgren, P. Testsituation och kodningsteknek vid ett frustrationstest. *Pedagogisk-psykologiska problem* (Malmö, Sweden: Lärarhögskolan), 1964, No. 9. (b)

Sundgren, P. Lärarpersonlighet och lärarlämplighet: En undersokning av klasslärarkandidater. *Pedagogisk-psykologiska problem* (Malmö, Sweden: Lärarhögskolan), 1967, No. 47.

Sutcliffe, J. P. An appraisal of the Rosenzweig Picture-Frustration Study. *Australian Journal of Psychology,* 1955, *7,* 97–107.

Sutcliffe, J. P. A rejoinder to Rosenzweig. *Australian Journal of Psychology,* 1957, *9,* 91–92.

Sviland, M. A. P. Factors of adaptation and rehabilitation in home hemodialysis. *Dissertation Abstracts,* 1972, *32,* 4230B.

Swickard, D. L., and Spilka, B. Hostility expression among delinquents of minority and majority groups. *Journal of Consulting Psychology,* 1961, *25,* 216–220.

Syme, L. Personality characteristics and the alcoholic. *Quarterly Journal of Studies on Alcohol,* 1957, *18,* 288–301.

Szakács, Ferenc. Szociabilitás-mutatók projektív tesztekben [Sociability indices in projective tests]. *Magyar Pszichologiai Szemle,* 1968, *25,* 564–578.

Szudra, E. Der Rosenzweig Picture-Frustration Test und seine Eignung für die klinische Psychodiagnostik des Kindesalters. *Monatsschrift für Kinderheilkunde,* 1966, *114,* 507–511.

Taft, R. Is the tolerant personality type the opposite of the intolerant? *Journal of Social Psychology,* 1958, *47,* 397–405.

Taft, R. Creativity: hot and cold. *Journal of Personality,* 1971, *39,* 345–361.

Takala, A., and Takala, M. Finnish children's reactions to frustration in the Rosenzweig test: an ethnic and cultural comparison. *Acta Psychologica,* 1957, *13,* 43–50.

Takala, M. Rosenzweig Picture-Frustration Study. In *Studies of psychomotor personality tests I.* Helsinki: Finnish Academy of Sciences, 1953, pp. 116–118.

Takala, M., Pihkanen, T. A., and Markkanen, T. *The effects of distilled and brewed beverages: a physiological, neurological and psychological study.* Helsinki: Finnish Foundation for Alcohol Studies, 1957, *4,* 118–188.

Tausch-Habeck, E. Der Erwachsene im Erlebnis des Kindes. *Zeitschrift für Experimentelle und Angewandte Psychologie,* 1956, *3,* 472–498.

Taylor, J. W. An experimental study of repression with special reference to success-failure and completion-incompletion. *Journal of Clinical Psychology,* 1953, *9,* 352–355.

Taylor, M. V., Jr. Internal consistency of the scoring categories of the Rosenzweig Picture-Frustration Study. *Journal of Consulting Psychology,* 1952, *16,* 149–153.

Taylor, M. V., Jr., and Taylor, O. M. Internal consistency of the Group Conformity Rating of the Rosenzweig Picture-Frustration Study. *Journal of Consulting Psychology,* 1951, *15,* 250–252.

TeBeest, D. L., and Dickie, J. R. Responses to frustration: comparison of institutionalized and noninstitutionalized retarded adolescents and nonretarded children and adolescents. *American Journal of Mental Deficiency,* 1976, *80,* 407–413.

Teichman, M. Ego defense, self-concept and image of self ascribed to parents by delinquent boys. *Perceptual and Motor Skills,* 1971, *32,* 819–823.

Temmer, H. W. An investigation into the effects of psychotherapy upon habitual avoidance and escape patterns displayed by delinquent adolescent girls. *Dissertation Abstracts,* 1958, *18,* 304.

Tewari, J. G., and Gautam, R. P. Personality characteristics of socially accepted and socially neglected junior high school pupils. *Indian Journal of Social Work,* 1966, *27,* 211–217.

Tewari, J. G., and Shukla, S. N. P-F and C.A.T. responses of the over- and under-chosen in the municipal primary school of Aligarh. *Indian Journal of Social Work,* 1968, *28,* 467–470.

Tewari, J. G., and Tewari, J. N. On extremes of personality adjustment as measured by adjustment inventories. *Journal of Psychological Researches,* 1968, *12,* 75–81.

Thaller, J. L., Rosen, G., and Saltzman, S. Study of the relationship of frustration and anxiety to bruxism. *Journal of Periodontia,* 1967, *38,* 193–197.

Thiesen, J. W., and Meister, R. K. A laboratory investigation of measures of frustration tolerance of pre-adolescent children. *Journal of Genetic Psychology,* 1949, *75,* 277–291.

Timaeus, E., and Wolf, S. Untersuchungen über den Rosenzweig P-F Test. *Zeitschrift für Experimentelle und Angewandte Psychologie,* 1962, *9,* 352–360.

Trapp, E. P. Threat and direction of aggression. *Journal of Clinical Psychology,* 1959, *15,* 308–310.

Trentini, G. Analisi sperimentale sul "faking": un aspetto trascurato della validazione dei tests. *Contributi dell'Istituto di Psicologia* (Milan: Società Editrice Vita e Pensiero), 1961, *24.*

Trentini, G. Contributo sperimentale alla validazione del test di Rosenzweig. *Contributi dell'Istituto di Psicologia,* 1962, *25,* 255–271.

Trentini, G. La trasposizione filmica del "Picture Frustration Test" di S. Rosenzweig. *Ikon (Revue Internationale de Filmologie),* 1966, *16,* 45–51.

Trentini, G. La trasposizioni filmica del "Picture Frustration Test" di S. Rosenzweig. *Ikon*, 1968, *18*, 9–38.

Trentini, G. Settentrionali e meridionali in Italia: Pregiudizio etnico, canalizzazione dell' aggressività e percezione interpersonale. *Contributi dell' Istituto di Psicologia*, 1970, *30*, 443–493.

Trentini, G., and Muzio, G. B. Taratura del "reattivo filmico di frustrazione" nelle somministrazioni individuale e di gruppo e reazioni ad esse secondo vari livelli di geografia socio-economico-culturale. *Ikon*, 1970, *20*, 39–82.

Triandis, L. M., and Lambert, W. W. Sources of frustration and targets of aggression: a cross-cultural study. *Journal of Abnormal and Social Psychology*, 1961, *62*, 640–648.

Tridenti, A., Ragionieri, M., Rigamonti, P. O., and de Risio, C. Investigation into the personality of patients with gastric and duodenal ulcer by means of the Rorschach and Rosenzweig tests. *Rivista Sperimentale di Freniatria e Medicina Legale delle Alienazioni Mentali*, 1972, *96*, 1400–1428.

Van Dam, F. Résultats d'une utilisation du test P.F. de Rosenzweig en sélection d'agents de vente. *Revue de Psychologie et des Sciences de l'Education*, 1970, *5*, 172–188.

Van Roy, F. *L'Enfant infirme, son handicap, son drame, sa guerison.* Paris: Delachaux & Niestle S.A., 1954. See Part Two, Chapters III and IV.

Vane, J. R. Implications of the performance of delinquent girls on the Rosenzweig Picture-Frustration Study. *Journal of Consulting Psychology*, 1954, *18*, 414.

Vieira, M. V. M., Machado, D. M., de Oliveira Pereira, A., and Litman, H. Características do teste GF-Rosenzweig em tuberculosos hospitalizados. *Arquivos Brasileiros de Psicologia Aplicada*, 1973, *25*, 51–124.

Villerbu, L. La formation de la résistance à la frustration et l'importance du contrôle de soi dans cet apprentissage. *L'Information Psychologique*, 1967, *25*, 35–36.

Villerbu, L. Examin critique du Picture Frustration Study de S. Rosenzweig. Ph.D. dissertation, Université de Nice, 1969.

Vinacke, W. E. A comparison of the Rosenzweig P-F Study and the Brown interracial version: Hawaii. *Journal of Social Psychology*, 1959, *49*, 161–175.

Viney, L. Reactions to frustration in chronically disabled patients. *Journal of Clinical Psychology*, 1972, *28*, 164–165.

Volle, F. O. &'Spilka, B. Hostility expression and stress-produced blood pressure variation. *American Psychologist*, 1961, 16, 352. (Abstract)

Walker, R. G. A comparison of clinical manifestations of hostility with Rorschach and MAPS Test performances. *Journal of Projective Techniques*, 1951, *15*, 444–460.

Wallen, N. E., Samuelson, C. O., Brewer, J. J., Gerber, S. K., and Woolaver, J. N. A comparison of slightly and severely orthopedically disabled and "normal" adults on several psychological tests. *Rehabilitation Counseling Bulletin*, 1964, *8*, 50–57.

Wallon, E. J. A study of Rosenzweig scoring patterns among naval aviation cadets. Bureau of Medicine and Surgery Research Project No. NM 001 109 100, Report No. 9. Pensacola, FL: U.S. Naval School of Aviation Medicine, Naval Air Station, May 1, 1956.

Wallon, E. J., and Webb, W. B. The effect of varying degrees of projection on test scores. *Journal of Consulting Psychology*, 1957, *21*, 465–472.

Watson, R. I. The Rosenzweig Picture-Frustration Study. Chapter 15 in *The clinical method in psychology*. New York: Harper, 1951.

Waugh, D. B. Attempted suicide and aggression: a study of three personality types of suicide attempters. *Dissertation Abstracts*, 1974, *35*, 1398B.

Weatherly, J. K. A comparative investigation of frustration-aggression patterns shown by adults and children within the same families of three religious groups. *Dissertation Abstracts*, 1966, *27*, 975.

Wechsberg, F. O. An experimental investigation of levels of behavior with special reference to the Rosenzweig Picture-Frustration Study. Unpublished doctoral dissertation, Washington University (St. Louis), 1951. Summarized in Rosenzweig, 1960, pp. 166–168.

Weiner, I. B., and Ader, R. Direction of aggression and adaptation to free operant avoidance conditioning. *Journal of Personality and Social Psychology*, 1965, *2*, 426–429.

Weinstein, A. D., Moore, C. W., and McCary, J. L. A note on the comparison of differences between several religious groups of adults on various measures of the Rosenzweig Picture-Frustration Study. *Journal of Clinical Psychology,* 1963, *19,* 219.

Weise, M. Der Rosenzweig-Picture-Frustration-Test bei Kindern mit leichtem hirnorganischen Residualsyndrom. *Praxis der Kinderpsychologie und Kinderpsychiatrie,* 1971, *20,* 170–172.

Weiss, W., and Fine, B. The effect of induced aggressiveness on opinion change. *Journal of Abnormal and Social Psychology,* 1956, *52,* 109–114.

Wendland, L. V. A preliminary study of frustration reactions of the post-poliomyelitic. *Journal of Clinical Psychology,* 1954, *10,* 236–240.

Werner, S. Versuch einer Objektivierung des Rosenzweig P-F tests. *Zeitschrift für Experimentelle und Angewandte Psychologie,* 1966, *13,* 133–155.

Wessman, A. E., Ricks, D. F., and Tyl, M. McI. Characteristics and concomitants of mood fluctuation in college women. *Journal of Abnormal and Social Psychology,* 1960, *60,* 117–126.

Whetstone, B. D. Personality differences between selected counselors and effective teachers. *Personnel and Guidance Journal,* 1965, *43,* 886–890.

White, W. C., Jr. Selective modeling in youthful offenders with high and low (overcontrolled-hostility) personality types. *Dissertation Abstracts,* 1971, *31,* 5648B.

Whitman, J. R., and Schwartz, A. N. Relationship between social desirability scale values and probability of endorsement in social situations. *Journal of Projective Techniques and Personality Assessment,* 1966, *30,* 280–282.

Whitman, J. R., and Schwartz, A. N. The relationship between two measures of the tendency to give socially desirable responses. *Journal of Projective Techniques and Personality Assessment,* 1967, *31,* 72–75.

Williams, S. G. Temporal experience and schizophrenia: a study of time orientation, attitude, and perspective. *Dissertation Abstracts,* 1965, *26,* 6862.

Wilson, G. D. Projective aggression and social attitudes. *Psychological Reports,* 1973, *32,* 1015–1018.

Wilson, M. E., Jr., and Frumkin, R. M. Underlying assumptions of the Rosenzweig Picture-Frustration Study: a critical appraisal. *Educational and Psychological Measurement,* 1968, *28,* 587–594.

Winfield, D. L., and Sparer, P. J. Preliminary report of the Rosenzweig P-F Study in attempted suicides. *Journal of Clinical Psychology,* 1953, *9,* 379–381.

Winslow, C. N., and Brainerd, J. E. A comparison of the reactions of whites and Negroes to frustration as measured by the Rosenzweig Picture-Frustration Test. *American Psychologist,* 1950, *5,* 297. (Abstract.)

Wittenborn, J. R., Dempster, A., Maurer, H., and Plante, M. Pretreatment of individual differences as potential predictors of response to pharmacology. *Journal of Nervous and Mental Disease,* 1964, *139,* 186–194.

Wittenborn, J. R., and Plante, M. Patterns of response to placebo, iproniazid and electroconvulsive therapy among young depressed females. *Journal of Nervous and Mental Disease,* 1963, *137,* 155–161.

Wittenborn, J. R., Plante, M., Burgess, F., and Livermore, N. The efficacy of electroconvulsive therapy, iproniazid and placebo in the treatment of young depressed women. *Journal of Nervous and Mental Disease,* 1961, *113,* 316–332.

Wolfgang, M. E., and Ferracuti, F. *The subculture of violence: toward an integrated theory in criminology.* London: Tavistock Publications, 1967.

Wright, J. M., and Harvey, O. J. Attitude change as a function of authoritarianism and punitiveness. *Journal of Personality and Social Psychology,* 1965, *1,* 177–181.

Wright, M. R., and McCary, J. L. Positive effects of sex information on emotional patterns of behavior. *Journal of Sex Research,* 1969, *5,* 162–169.

Zaidi, S. M. H., and Shafi, K. An objective evaluation of Rosenzweig's analysis of subjective reactions to frustration in a Pakistani cultural setting. *Psychologia: An International Journal of Psychology in the Orient,* 1965, *8,* 213–217.

Zimet, S. G., Rose, C., and Camp, B. W. Relationship between reading achievement and Rosenzweig Picture-Frustration Study in early grades. *Psychology in the Schools,* 1973, *10,* 433–436.

Zubin, J., Eron, L. D., & Schumer, F. *An experimental approach to projective techniques.* New York: John Wiley, 1965, pp. 487–496.

Zuckerman, M. The effect of frustration on the perception of neutral and aggressive words. *Journal of Personality,* 1955, *23,* 407–422.

Zuk, G. H. The influence of social context on impulse and control tendencies in preadolescents. *Genetic Psychology Monographs,* 1956, *54,* 117–166.

Supplementary References

These references are not directly concerned with the P-F Study but have been cited in the text, as relevant, with author and date in italics.

Allport, G. W. A test for Ascendance-Submission. *Journal of Abnormal and Social Psychology*, 1928, *23*, 118–136.

American Psychological Association. *Standards for educational and psychological tests and manuals.* Washington, D.C.: American Psychological Association, 1966.

Blatt, S. J. The validity of projective techniques and their research and clinical contribution. *Journal of Personality Assessment*, 1975, *39*, 327–343.

Burgess, A. *A clockwork orange.* New York: Norton, 1963.

Cronbach, L. J. Validation of educational measures. *Proceedings of the 1969 Invitational Conference on Testing Problems.* Princeton, N.J.: Educational Testing Service, 1970, pp. 35–52.

Cronbach, L. J. Test validation. In R. L. Thorndike (Ed.). *Educational measurement* (2d ed.). Washington, D.C.: American Council on Education, 1971.

Dollard, J., Doob, L. W., Miller, N. E., Mowrer, O. H., and Sears, R. R. *Frustration and aggression.* New Haven: Yale University Press, 1939.

Frankenhaeuser, M., and Kareby, S. Effect of meprobamate on catecholamine excretion during mental stress. *Perceptual and Motor Skills*, 1962, *15*, 571–577.

Galton, F. Psychometric experiments. *Brain,* 1879–1880, *2,* 149–162.

Guilford, J. P. *Fundamental statistics in psychology and education* (2d ed.). New York: McGraw-Hill, 1950.

Hill, E. F. *The Holtzman Inkblot Technique.* San Francisco: Jossey-Bass, 1972.

Hokfelt, B. Noradrenaline and adrenaline in mammalian tissues. *Acta Physiologica Scandinavica,* 1951, *25,* Suppl. 92, 5–134.

Holtzman, W. H., Thorpe, J. S., Swartz, J. D., and Herron, E. W. *Inkblot perception and personality.* Austin: University of Texas Press, 1961.

Jung, C. G. *Studies in word association.* English translation. London: Heinemann, 1918. (German edition, 1906.)

Kubrick, S. *A clockwork orange.* New York: Ballantine Books, 1972. (Screenplay)

Lake, D. G., Miles, M. B., and Earle, R. B., Jr. *Measuring human behavior: tools for the assessment of social functioning.* New York: Teachers College Press, 1973, pp. 295–300.

Macfarlane, J. W. Problems of validation inherent in projective methods. *American Journal of Orthopsychiatry,* 1942, *12,* 405–410.

Messick, S. The standard problem. *American Psychologist,* 1975, *30,* 955–966.

Mischel, W. *Personality and assessment.* New York: John Wiley, 1968.

Morgan, C. D., and Murray, H. A. A method for investigating phantasies: the Thematic Apperception Test. *Archives of Neurology and Psychiatry,* 1935, *34,* 289–306.

Rosenzweig, S. Philosophy and psychoanalysis. A study in the reciprocal relationships between two parallel schools: Schopenhauer, Freud; Nietzsche, Adler; Bergson, Jung. Unpublished honors thesis, Harvard University, 1929.

Schildkraut, J. J. and Kety, S. S. Biogenic amines and emotion. *Science* 1967, *156,* 21–30.

Silverman, A. J., Cohen, S. I., Zuidema, G. D., and Lazar, C. S. Prediction of physiological stress tolerance from projective tests: "The focused Thematic Test." *Journal of Projective Techniques,* 1957, *21,* 189–193.

NAME INDEX

Names of authors whose work is discussed in the text are indexed here. Additional names will be found in the Citation Index and the References by Author.

SUBJECT INDEX

Entries such as Administration, Reliability, Validity, etc. are to be read with P-F Study implied as a prior heading unless otherwise stated.